P9-APZ-191

DONALD CAPPS

DEADLY SINS
AND
SAVING VIRTUES

FORTRESS PRESS   **PHILADELPHIA**

Biblical quotations, unless otherwise noted, are from the Revised Standard Version of the Bible, copyright 1946, 1952, © 1971, 1973 by the Division of Christian Education of the National Council of the Churches of Christ in the U.S.A., and are used by permission.

COPYRIGHT © 1987 BY FORTRESS PRESS

All rights reserved. No part of this publication may be reproduced, stored in a retrieval system, or transmitted in any form or by any means, electronic, mechanical, photocopying, recording, or otherwise, without the prior permission of the copyright owner.

Library of Congress Cataloging-in-Publication Data

Capps, Donald.
   Deadly sins and saving virtues.

   Bibliography: p.
   1. Deadly sins. 2. Virtues. 3. Life cycle,
Human—Religious aspects—Christianity. 4. Pastoral
psychology. 5. Pastoral counseling. I. Title.
BV4626.C37 1987   241'.3   86–45912
ISBN 0–8006–1948–X

2649G86   Printed in the United States of America   1–1948

To John

The father of the righteous will greatly rejoice;
  he who begets a wise son will be glad in him.
Let your father and mother be glad,
  let her who bore you rejoice.

(Prov. 23:24–25)

Contents

Acknowledgments   vi

Introduction   1

PART ONE. The Deadly Sins

1. The Traditional Deadly Sins   11
2. The Sins of Infancy and Early Childhood   21
3. The Sins of the Play Age and School Age   33
4. The Sins of Adolescence and Young Adulthood   46
5. The Sins of Middle and Mature Adulthood   58

PART TWO. The Saving Virtues

6. The Virtues of Infancy and Early Childhood   73
7. The Virtues of Childhood and Adolescence   87
8. The Virtues of Adulthood   101

PART THREE. The Saving Graces

9. The Beatitudes—Elements of an Active Faith   119
10. Biblical Stories and the Pilgrim's Way   137

Notes   153

Index   159

Acknowledgments

The major themes of this book have been presented in lectures and talks to various groups, including chaplains, psychiatrists and mental-health workers, parish clergy, pastoral counselors, seminary and university students, and church laity. I have learned a great deal from the conversations these presentations afforded, and wish to thank those individuals whose suggestions and observations have been incorporated into the book. I am also grateful to various members of the Fortress Press staff, especially Harold Rast, who supported this project, Thelma Megill-Cobbler, who made many valuable editorial suggestions, and Barry Blose, who did the copy editing. My thanks go also to Thomas W. Gillespie, President of Princeton Theological Seminary, for fostering an institutional climate conducive to faculty research and writing, and I owe a debt of special appreciation to Ann Hoch for preparing the index.

This book is dedicated to our teenage son, John, who prepared the penultimate draft of the manuscript on his computer. Agatha Christie has said that writing is murder. If so, John was an indispensable accomplice.

Introduction

Are certain sins more serious than other sins? It is a view widely held among Christian theologians that although no sin is a trivial matter, certain sins are worse than others. One of the most popular developments from the conviction that some sins are more serious than others is the concept of the deadly sins. This concept goes back at least as far as the fourth century of the Christian era. It is a concept that says that certain sins place us in greater spiritual jeopardy than others do.

The present book is about those deadly sins. It focuses on the traditional list of deadly sins and finds them as "deadly" today as they have ever been in the history of the Christian faith. To understand why they are especially deadly, we first need to explain what we mean by sin. For the purposes of this study, sin is an orientation to life which is potentially or actually harmful in one or more of the following ways:

1. The orientation to life is an impediment or threat to human community. Here, human community includes every form of human interaction, including close interpersonal relationships, small groups and informal alliances, institutions, and national and international relations.

2. The orientation to life is an impediment to God's own intentions for the world, including the world of human society and the world of nature. The orientation either knowingly or unwittingly frustrates God's intentions for the world, and it evidences no disposition to ascertain what those intentions may be either in the long run or in specific, immediate contexts and situations.

3. The orientation to life inhibits and even destroys the essential

1

well-being of the individual. By well-being, I have in mind the health or wholeness of the individual in the various interrelated domains of personal existence: the psychological (including one's emotional, perceptual, and cognitive life), the physiological, the interpersonal, the societal (which involves one's relationship to human community as a whole), and that of the spiritual health of the individual (which involves one's sense of living "in concert" with God and God's intentions for the world). Usually a sin that threatens one of these intentionalities also threatens the others. A sense of personal well-being cannot be sustained, at least for long, where human community and God's intentions for the world are under siege.

By emphasizing that sin is an orientation to life, we avoid the suggestion that sin is purely a matter of action or behavior. Any orientation to life may range from a relatively permanent *disposition* to life, to an *attitude* that is relatively amenable to change, to a transitory *impulse*, which is the most unstable orientation of all. Actions issue from all three sorts of orientation. We act on dispositions, attitudes, and impulses.

In my judgment, certain sins have been judged to be deadly because they are very likely to become dispositional, and thus relatively permanent features of an individual's orientation to life. When we confess on Sunday morning that we are "in bondage to sin," we are acknowledging a sinful disposition. The dictionary, for example, defines a disposition as a "normal or prevailing aspect of one's nature," as, for example, a "genial disposition." Thus, certain sins are more deadly than others because they are more likely to become dispositional in nature, disposing us toward a sinful orientation to life.

A major premise of this book is that, if sin is dispositional, it is intrinsic to the developmental process itself. As we as individuals grow and mature, certain dispositions toward life emerge and become relatively permanent aspects of our personalities. Since the Christian tradition says that we are born children of a fallen humanity, a disposition toward sinfulness is inherent in us from the very beginning. But the specific forms this disposition will take begin to unfold as we develop, from infancy to childhood to adulthood. It is here that the traditional formulation of the deadly sins is very helpful, because it suggests that the disposition to sinfulness is multidimensional. It suggests that there are at least seven basic forms that our disposition to sinfulness can take and that these forms may come to be related to one another in very complex ways.

The central argument of this book is that the basic forms of the disposition to sin are directly related to the stages of the life cycle. At each stage of life, we are disposed toward a particular deadly sin and are tempted to orient ourselves to life in the terms of this deadly sin. The disposition to sinfulness is inherent in us from the very beginning of our existence, but the disposition toward a specific sin occurs at a specific stage of the life cycle. Then, once this disposition has come into being, it remains a potentially powerful influence on us throughout our lives. The major point of this book is that dispositions are related to development and, thus, that dispositions to sin follow a developmental pattern or sequence.

To make this point and to explore its implications, I draw on the developmental theory formulated by Erik H. Erikson. His is perhaps the best-known developmental theory available today. It serves our needs especially well because, unlike many other developmental theories, it spans the whole life cycle, from birth to death. Furthermore, it suggests that there are identifiable "crisis points" in the developmental process, with the crises setting the stage for movement into the next stage of life. The crisis points are important for our purposes here, because with each crisis we are confronted with the task of reorienting our lives, of relating to the world around us in new and different ways. (This is not primarily the consequence of social demands, though they are certainly a factor. The more decisive factors are physiological changes and the emotional, perceptual, and cognitive responses and adjustments that the physiological changes require.)

I am arguing, therefore, that at each of the crisis points in life, we are under considerable pressure to orient ourselves to life in terms of the deadly sin I have assigned to that particular stage. In a sense, we are more vulnerable at the crisis points to the influence of sin, in the dispositional sense, because we are at that point needing to reorient ourselves to life and are under considerable pressure to overcome the disorienting effects of the crisis in which we find ourselves. The major contribution of this book is that it links specific deadly sins to specific life stages, thereby alerting us to the nature of the sin to which we are likely to be disposed at each stage in life.

But this is only half the story that the book seeks to tell. The other half—the more positive side—involves the contention that, even as we are disposed toward certain sins at given stages of the life cycle, we are also disposed toward certain virtues. In contrast to the deadly sins, these virtues—which I call saving virtues—orient us toward life in ways that enhance human community of every kind, enable us to discern God's intentions for the world and to contribute to their realization, and contribute to our personal well-being in its various interrelated aspects.

The virtues identified in this study are "saving" because they are likely to be more than impulses or even attitudes and to become enduring dispositions toward life. And because they dispose us to the orientation to life opposite that of the deadly sins, they are directly opposed to the deadly sins. Sometimes, we are conscious of this opposition in the world or in ourselves, and when that is the case, we often use conflict language to describe it. In the Christian tradition, language reminiscent of military battles has often been employed (e.g., there are references to sin as enemy, to conquering sin, to achieving the victory over sin, to defeating the agents of sin, and so forth). Though military imagery may be disagreeable in some ways, it serves to underscore the fact that the conflict is a serious one, for nothing less than our ultimate orientation to life is at stake here.

As with sin, the disposition toward virtue is inherent. Our tendency toward virtue is not merely a matter of personal will or positive nurturance. It is a God-given capacity. The claim that we are created in the image of God is one way in which Christians have accounted for the inherent tendency toward virtue. By accounting for it in this way, we make the point that virtue is more than a moral capacity; it is also, and more fundamentally, a capacity for spiritual growth and discernment, especially for the discernment of God's intentions for the world.

The saving virtues are those that are likely to effect enduring dispositions toward life. And following Erikson himself, I contend that the saving virtues are related to the developmental process. At each crisis point in our development, there is a saving virtue (or two) which becomes available to provide us with an orientation to life quite the opposite of the orientation provided by the corresponding deadly sin. Erikson has himself proposed a "schedule of virtues" corresponding to the stages in his life-cycle theory. In discussing the saving virtues and their role in contesting the deadly sins, I will be using his formulation, with some additions of my own.

Perhaps an explanation is in order concerning my use of the term "saving" virtue. I do not intend to make a theological statement by adopting the term—that is, to imply that we are saved "by works" or by our own moral efforts. I use the term "saving" virtue in the more popular sense, as when we say that an individual's kindness to everyone she met was her saving virtue. In this sense, a virtue is a disposition toward life, a characteristic way of relating to the world around us. Saving virtues thus offer a clear alternative to the deadly sins, because they are no less dispositional and are therefore just as capable of shaping our orientation to life. A major contribution of this book is that, following Erikson, it identifies the specific disposition to virtue that occurs at each stage of the life cycle. As with the deadly sins, each disposition survives the stage in which it becomes of critical importance, but it retains its close identification with the crisis of that stage and with the orientation to life which emerged out of that crisis.

There is one additional element of the book's argument that requires mention at the outset. A major premise of the study is that the disposition to virtue, although inherent, can be cultivated: there are things that individuals and societies can do to foster the disposition to virtue. Many different methods, projects, programs, and resources have been formulated and employed throughout human history for the purpose of cultivating the virtues and thus reinforcing the disposition of individuals toward a virtuous orientation to life. Some of the methods and programs have had their intended effect; others have failed or have even proved counterproductive (i.e., they have contributed to an orientation toward sinfulness). The cultivation of virtue has been fostered, however, through direct teaching and exhortation, through the personal example of significant others, through social institutions, orders, agencies, and movements dedicated to the enhancement of human community, and through countless other means.

This book too is concerned with the cultivation of virtue, drawing attention to the Bible as a major resource for assisting individuals and groups in the nurturing of a virtuous orientation to life and, more specifically, of a life reflecting the saving virtues. Here the Bible is not construed as merely a moral book, or a book that teaches and advocates morality. Instead it is appropriated for the purpose of cultivating virtue in the larger and deeper sense already indicated (as enhancing human community, discerning and supporting God's intentions for the world, and contributing to personal well-being).

The Bible is used here in three different ways. First, by using stories of some significant biblical figures in the Old Testament, I draw attention to the conflict of deadly sin versus saving virtue in each stage of the life cycle. Thus, the biblical stories illustrate the basic problem to which the study is addressed: the fact that the dispositions to sinfulness and to virtue are both inherent in us. As regards our orientation to life, we are continually being pulled in opposing directions. In my judgment, it is illuminating and even reassuring to know that others have been as torn between the deadly sins and the saving virtues as we are. Through these examples, I hope to provide the reader with a lively sense of how sin, as disposition, is an impediment to human community, to the intentions of God for the world, and to the well-being of the individual; and how virtue, as disposition, contributes to human community, discerns and helps to realize God's intentions for the world, and helps to secure and foster the well-being of the individual.

The biblical examples also illustrate how individuals experiencing crisis points in their lives are faced with two basic orientations to life—the way of sinfulness and the way of virtue. None of the figures discussed in this study resolved this crisis in an unambiguous way. None was without a disposition to sin, or without the disposition to virtue. But for some the crisis led to a clear intent to orient their lives according to virtue (Esau, Balaam, Koheleth, and Job). For another, the crisis led to an equally clear intent to orient his life to sin (Saul). For still others, the biblical story paints a cloudy picture (Moses, Samson) or leaves the ultimate outcome in doubt (Jonah).

Second, by focusing on the Beatitudes of Jesus and linking them to the developmental process, I draw attention to Jesus' vision of "active faith" and show how that vision may inspire and foster the disposition toward virtue. The Beatitudes are very important to the whole orientation of my study because they can be viewed as providing a normative vision of human community, of God's intentions for the world, and of personal well-being. That vision energizes the disposition to virtue and challenges the disposition to sinfulness. And even more specifically, individual beatitudes undergird the saving virtues to which they are related in the developmental cycle. Thus, the discussion of the Beatitudes enables us to view active faith as multidimensional and not unidimensional (as though faith has no discernible characteristics or identifiable elements). The function of the Beatitudes in this study is therefore to draw attention to the relationship between faith and virtue, and to ground the virtuous orientation to life in a conception of faith that has clearly identifiable elements (not in a conception of faith as a vague abstraction). In much Christian theologizing about faith, a dichotomy is established between faith and virtue. By linking the Beatitudes to the saving virtues, I am attempting to undermine this dichotomy and to challenge the kind of thinking that gives rise to such dichotomies.

Third, I draw attention to the pilgrimage motif as developed in the Bible and extended by John Bunyan in *The Pilgrim's Progress*. I focus on this motif because I believe that it addresses our need for an orientation in life but also recognizes that such an orientation cannot be one in which we remain immobile and unchanging. The pilgrim motif supports the disposition to virtue and thus provides a grounding for a virtuous orientation to life, one that pursues human community, that attempts to discern and operate in concert with God's intentions for the world, and that recognizes our personal need (often desperate) for essential well-being. The pilgrim motif also takes seriously the contest between the dispositions to sin and to virtue, recognizing that the contest is both intrapsychic and societal. The pilgrim motif undergirds a developmental understanding of the contest in that it conceives the journey of life as a series of crisis points that threaten our basic orientation to life and challenge us to reorient ourselves to the world around us.

The pilgrim motif is only one biblical metaphor for envisioning the course of our lives. But for this study its importance is in the fact that it offers a conception of a virtuous orientation to life that takes seriously the fact that we are ever changing, always in motion, and rarely at rest. As I will attempt to show, the pilgrimage motif is congruent with Erikson's developmental theory, not only in that it coheres with Erikson's emphasis on crisis points and stages of life but also, and more fundamentally, in that for both the pilgrimage motif and the life-cycle theory, the orientation is provided by future anticipations and goals, not by the point of origin. Both are forward-looking.

These three uses of the biblical tradition are only three of the many possible ways in which the Bible may be a resource for cultivating the saving virtues and challenging the deadly sins. In earlier writings, I have pointed out that the deadly sins and saving virtues, and their interrelationships, are of great concern to the biblical wisdom tradition, especially the Book of Proverbs.[1] There would be equal value in an examination of New Testament images of the church that showed how the church's own self-understanding offers an important vision of the virtuous orientation to life (the way of salvation). It would also be worthwhile to follow up chapter 10's discussion of biblical women (Naomi and Ruth), using the biblical stories of women, children, and demoniacs to focus on the fate of innocent victims of the deadly sins.

PART ONE

THE DEADLY
SINS

CHAPTER ONE

The Traditional
Deadly Sins

The traditional "seven deadly sins" are portrayed in medieval literature like Dante's *Inferno* and Chaucer's *Canterbury Tales*. They have also been preached from the pulpit, taught in courses on moral philosophy, and warned against in the confessional. They are frequently employed in modern drama, poetry, mystery stories, and film. From time to time, the classification of the seven deadly sins has been the object of amusement and scorn. But just when it seems there is no longer any interest in the classification, it suddenly reappears and once again captures our interest and imagination.

Judging from the number of books recently published on the deadly sins, the classification is now enjoying a resurgence. The authors of these books believe that the traditional model of deadly sins remains a valuable vehicle for personal self-examination. Yet, even though much has been written on the deadly sins, few of us have any real knowledge about the traditional list, and most of us would have difficulty naming the sins it includes.

In this chapter, I will explain how the traditional list came about and then report on what is today being written about the deadly sins.

The Traditional List of Deadly Sins

Why Seven?

The traditional list includes seven deadly sins commonly given in the following order: pride, envy, anger, sloth, greed, gluttony, and lust.

In some of the earliest lists, dating back to the fourth century of the Christian era, there were eight, not seven, sins. Evagrius of Pontus listed eight. So did John of Cassian. Even Gregory the Great, who is primarily responsible for the current list of seven, had eight sins in his list. He considered pride the root of all sin, and then listed seven additional deadly sins.

Eventually the church settled on seven deadly sins and agreed on the order given above. The major omission from the original lists of eight is melancholy, or *tristitia*. It was merged with apathy, or *acedia*, and apathy came to be the accepted name for the combined sin until in English versions the sin was called sloth. There was also much debate over two other sins in the original list of eight, vainglory and pride. These were separate sins in Evagrius's list, but vainglory was later included in the sin of pride.

Why was the list reduced from eight to seven? One reason is that seven is a sacred number. There are the seven gifts of the Holy Spirit, the seven penitential psalms, the seven virtues, and the seven sorrows of the blessed virgin Mary.[1] But the seven-day week may also have had something to do with it. A list of seven sins would lend itself to daily prayer, with each day's prayer focusing on the sin assigned to it. This explanation is supported by the fact that an official order was adopted. Sunday is the day we combat *pride* by attending religious services and proclaiming God, not ourselves, as the center of our lives and of all creation. *Envy* and *anger* are Monday and Tuesday's sins because these sins involve injury to our personal worth and dignity and require a continuation of Sunday's struggle against pride. *Sloth*, Wednesday's sin, is most deadly at the midpoint of the week, when we are at greatest distance from the liturgy or "work of God" of the previous and approaching Sundays and therefore the most susceptible to spiritual indifference. *Greed* and *gluttony*, Thursday and Friday's sins, are the sins of self-indulgence that follow from the previous day's loss of spiritual fortitude. Traditionally, gluttony has been combated by fasting on Friday. These two sins culminate in *lust*, Saturday's sin, the most self-indulgent of all sins and deadliest on the last day of the week, when the spiritual effects of Sunday's day of worship are at their lowest ebb. Thus, quite possibly the deadly sins were reduced to seven and placed in the order we have them now so as to correspond with the days of the week.

A Dynamic System

Throughout history, there have been many attempts to group or cluster two or more of the deadly sins. Gluttony and greed are commonly linked because both involve the desire for more of something than we need or should desire. Envy is also linked with greed because both sins involve wanting something that someone else possesses. Lust and sloth are often linked because it is felt that work is an antidote to sexual promiscuity. Lust and anger are commonly linked because they both involve strong emotions temporarily out of control. Lust is also linked with greed because lust is considered a stimulus to greed.

The linkings are often described in terms of family relationships. Gluttony may be said to be the brother of greed, or lust the cousin of sloth. Or they are described in parent-child terms, thus making possible the claim that two sins may produce a third, as when envy and greed are said to be the parents of anger. Or a parent sin may be said to give birth to two or more sins, as when sloth is said to be the parent of gluttony and lust.

Through the use of the family metaphor, the deadly sins are often personified. They are spelled with a capital first letter and referred to as active agents, as though they and not we enact or perform the forbidden act. This use of the family metaphor sees the sins as dynamically related, forming what modern family therapists call dyadic and triadic relationships within a family system.

No doubt every single sin has been linked to every other sin. But this does not invalidate the cluster concept. Clustering is a better principle for relating the deadly sins to one another than the idea, put forward by John of Cassian, that each sin grows out of the previous one. That chain of causality seems contrived and artificial. The idea that certain sins are dynamically related is more convincing. In this view, the deadly sins are a dynamic system similar to the extended family with its various nuclear families, or to a large nuclear family.

What about the deadly sins' relationship to other sins? The most common metaphor for portraying the connection is the tree and its branches. In "The Parson's Tale," one of the *Canterbury Tales*, Chaucer describes the seven deadly sins as the "trunk of the tree from which others branch."[2] With this metaphor, other sins are not disregarded but are viewed as extensions of the deadly sins.

The Deadly Sins as Personal Fault

What do we mean when we call the deadly sins "sins"? And why are these considered more "deadly" than other sins? Recent books address both of these questions. On the first question, some authors view the deadly sins as personal faults, while others view them as social evil. On the second question, there is much debate at the present time over whether the seven are in fact the deadliest of all sins. Let us look at the first question first.

In *Whatever Became of Sin?* Karl Menninger lamented the fact that we no longer talk about sin and guilt. What our forebears called sin, we call behavioral problems. What they called guilt, we call emotional distress. The language of sin has been replaced by the language of symptom. In challenging us to recover the language of sin, Menninger devotes a chapter to "The Old Seven Deadly Sins (And Some New Ones)."[3] To him, the traditional deadly sins are no less relevant today than they were to our ancestors. And they are deadly because they are terribly difficult to get rid of once they have taken hold of us. Like a deadly cancer, they are a wasting disease that spreads, expands, and takes on new forms. Lust is joined by other sins of sensuality, including fornication, adultery, and pornography. Anger is expanded into violence and aggression. Envy and greed spawn avarice and affluence. Then other sins appear, including waste, cheating, stealing, lying, and cruelty. Engendered by the deadly sins, these sins develop independent lives of their own.

Menninger does not want to subscribe to an official list of sins. Nor does he want to focus exclusively on sinful behavior. Instead, his interest centers on the *attitudes* that give rise to sinful behavior. The deadly sins and the sins they breed "are forms of behavior resulting from sinful intent or neglect. They are samples of the behavior dictated by a wrong attitude, a hard heart, a cold heart, an evil heart." The deadly sins, like all sins, have their source in attitudes, in habits of the heart.

In a chapter on "Sin and Sickness" in *Theological Dynamics*, Seward Hiltner makes a similar plea for attention to the deadly sins. He notes that Protestants have tried to avoid any classification of sins, on the grounds that all sins are equally hateful in God's sight. But he believes that "some degree of classification is inevitable, and that the question is whether it will be on sound grounds, flexible and supported by hard data on how small beginnings do or do not lead to dire consequences."[4]

Hiltner has mixed feelings about the list of seven deadly sins. On the one hand, if an attempt is made to compile "a neat assortment of really serious sins, anybody with enough brains could figure out how to keep his own propensities out of the list." On the other hand, the traditional list focuses not on isolated acts but on the tendencies of repetition, and these cannot be so easily manipulated or disguised: "Acts are not absent, but they are implied to be inevitable consequences of tendencies of character." This means that the list of deadly sins relates sin to personality dynamics. The connection with personality dynamics is lost when we talk only about sin with a capital *S*. The naming of sins enables us to explore the dynamic roots of sin and to recognize that different sins have different effects on personality and character formation. In linking sins to personality dynamics, Hiltner identifies several metaphors for sin. The three most influential of these in the history of the Christian faith see sin as rebellion, as missing the mark, and as isolation. Each has an implied dynamic, with rebellion connoting aggressiveness, missing the mark implying personal bondage, and isolation focusing on alienation and estrangement. Later we will see that these three root metaphors are useful for identifying clusters of the deadly sins, for some deadly sins are more closely associated with aggression, others with personal bondage, and still others with estrangement. In later discussion, I will identify the second metaphor as personal bondage, not as missing the mark, because I believe personal bondage more adequately captures the underlying dynamic of that form of sin.

With their commitment to religion and psychiatry, Menninger and Hiltner are most concerned with the underlying dynamics of the deadly sins. They view the deadly sins not as isolated behaviors but as dynamic tendencies and inner dispositions of the individual. In contrast to the authors whom I will discuss next, they focus mainly on the effects of the deadly sins *on individuals*. Though they are certainly aware of corporate sin, their main focus is on sin as personal, not collective, fault.

The Deadly Sins as Social Evil

Two contemporary writers, Stanford Lyman and Kenneth Slack, are especially concerned with the society that tolerates and even positively values the deadly sins. Lyman takes a social-evil approach to the deadly sins, calling his investigations into the deadly sins a "study in the sociology of evil." He criticizes modern sociology for relegating evil to the study of deviance, and he wants to "return sociology to the *topic* of evil in its own right." It disturbs him that evil gets depersonalized in modern society. We have created great corporate structures, empowered them with money, endowed them with strength and potency, and freed them from personal, social, or moral responsibility. In times past, the workplace was considered a moral context, keeping the worker from the temptations of pride, avarice, envy, and gluttony; coercing the worker away from sloth; reducing and controlling lust;

and chastening anger. Now, however, the modern corporation has neutralized sin, liberating its employees from personal, social, and moral responsibility.

In chapters devoted to each of the seven deadly sins, Lyman discusses their social manifestations and their effects on society. In each case, he describes their unmitigated evil form but also explores their beneficent effects when sublimated, chastened, or redirected. For example, he notes that when pride is sublimated as honor, dignity, or self-confidence, it serves as a sign of morality, a surety of character, and an incentive to succeed.[5]

In his book on the deadly sins, Slack shares Lyman's view that the deadly sins reflect social pathology. He criticizes societies that indulge in national pride when they argue that "we" are inherently better than "they." And he points out that corporate gluttony and greed are reflected in the energy crisis and our misuse of natural resources.[6]

Thus, for Lyman and Slack the deadly sins are not just personal faults but also great social evils. They influence the social structures and processes of a society and produce sick societies.

The Traditional List: How Adequate?

How adequate is the traditional list of seven deadly sins? Does it include the deadliest of sins? Two contemporary authors who address this question are Judith Shklar and Mary Daly.[7] Shklar does not attack the traditional list, but she questions whether it identifies the worst personal and social evils. In her judgment the traditional deadly sins do reflect the abysses of human character. But she chooses to focus instead on a more subtle but no less dangerous set of evils, what Montaigne called ordinary vices. These are vices that have become so commonplace that they raise no eyebrows among ordinary citizens and receive scant attention from moral philosophers. But they are the stuff of novelists, dramatists, and poets. The ordinary vices include cruelty, hypocrisy, snobbery, betrayal, and misanthropy—and chief among them is cruelty. Menninger insisted that cruelty belongs in contemporary discussions of sin, especially cruelty to children and animals and the infliction of psychological pain through name-calling and psychiatric labeling. Shklar shares this view. With Montaigne, she emphasizes that cruelty is the ultimate source of all the other ordinary vices: cruelty produces hypocrisy, snobbery, treachery, and misanthropy.

For Shklar, the ordinary vices are reflections of a whole society. They "create individuals from whom we may shrink for any number of quite different personal or shared reasons. When we think of these vices, however, we must do what the tradition of character writers did: relate the vice bearer to a whole social and religious scheme."[8] Classifications of sin produced by any society are themselves a reflection of the moral distortions of that society. For modern society, Shklar prefers Montaigne's list of ordinary vices to the model of the seven deadly sins because the traditional list emphasizes the sins of pride and self-indulgence but the model of ordinary vices puts cruelty first. In her judgment, cruelty is today a more deadly form of social pathology than either pride or self-indulgence. On the other hand, she concludes her study with the observation that today we "have no need for simple lists of vices and virtues," for such lists imply that there is some agreement among the members of a society about what constitutes sins and virtues. She contends that it is the very nature of democratic, pluralistic societies that such agreement is neither sought nor desired. The value of simple lists is that they "reveal what we have to contend with"—that is, they help us to identify at least some of our personal and social pathologies. But they should not be thought of as complete or universally agreed upon.

Daly shares Shklar's view that the traditional list of deadly sins reflects the moral preoccupations and distortions of the society that produced it. She contends that the list is the "perverted paradigm" of patriarchal society, and therefore suspect for two reasons. First, it centers on the temptations to which men are especially subject. Women's lists of deadly sins would undoubtedly look quite different, even antithetical to men's. What is a sin for a man may well be a virtue for a woman. Second, descriptions of the sins have been developed mainly by men and are therefore the product of men's partial and distorted perspective on these very sins. Men who describe the deadly sins are talking about their own sins. So why expect that they would depict them accurately? How can they discuss their own sins honestly? In Daly's opinion, men's views of these sins are based on self-deception.

The solution is for women to expose the deception behind the whole enterprise of listing the deadly sins. As the victims of the sins, women know that men do not in fact believe that these *are* deadly sins. Instead, the sins are the very core of men's system of values and are essential to the maintenance of their dominant position in the social world. Men's sanctimonious denunciations of the deadly sins are not to be believed, for men actually honor and reward pride, greed, anger, lust, gluttony, envy, and sloth. Thus, for Daly it is high time that women openly revealed what they have always known, that the deadly sins constitute men's code of virtue, whereas men's lists of virtues tell what they expect of women, so that men may continue to dominate them.

In short, women are the victims of men's deadly sins. *Pride* is epitomized in patriarchal professions that condense the process of knowing into an inert "body of knowledge." *Greed* (or avarice) is the demonic possession of female spirit and energy, accomplished not only through political and economic means but also, more deeply, through male myths about themselves. The malevolence of male violence is misnamed *anger* (unlike true anger, it is usually dispassionate); the deception allows the fact to be masked that women are the enemy against whom all patriarchal wars are waged, and it therefore mutes righteous female anger. Male *lust* specializes in genital fixation, generating false masculine and feminine role constructs. Male *gluttony* feeds on the living flesh, blood, and spirit of women. Male *envy* tends toward the elimination of all self-identified women. And patriarchal *sloth* has enslaved women, forcing them into subservient social activities resulting in "busy" and enforced feminine sloth.[9]

In my judgment, Daly is correct in her view that the traditional list of deadly sins is largely a reflection of a male-dominated society. But this does not mean that we should reject the traditional list. If anything, it means that we should take it even more seriously. However distorted and destructive its use has been, the list helps us to identify the sins prevailing in our society. And certainly Daly does not intend to exempt women from sin. Her point, rather, is that in a society where men are in power, women's sins will be reflections of male domination (e.g., women's "busyness" being a form of sloth).

Because my approach to the deadly sins is developmental, the primary focus of this book is on the deadly sins as personal fault. I will be exploring the deadly sins as personal dispositions or habits and will be giving particular attention to the dynamics of sin in the individual. But the view of sin as social evil can never be far from our considerations. For as Lyman and Slack make clear, the traditional list of deadly sins is a very useful construct for identifying the sins of our society and its institutional structures, and it thus enables us to discern the role that society, especially through its institutions, plays in the sinfulness of individuals. And as Shklar and Daly point out, the lists of sins developed by any society tell us a great deal about that society's fundamental values. In light of the fact that the traditional list of deadly sins has gained a kind of mass appeal in recent decades (i.e., has come out of the confessional and the class in moral philosophy and become a significant part of popular culture through novels, plays, and films), this list is a very useful construct for looking at sin as a cultural phenomenon. To the extent that we are as much a product of popular culture as of social institutions, the traditional list is helpful for discerning the role that our culture, in a more diffuse but yet very powerful way, plays in the sinfulness of individuals. This is not to say, of course, that individuals have no responsibility for their sinfulness. It is simply to emphasize that, though we will be focusing on the individual in this book, we need to keep constantly in mind the fact that the society in which we live and the culture whose spirit is all around us create an ethos in which certain sins are taken more seriously than others and some sins are not considered sinful at all.

The Saving Virtues

The working premise of this book is that the traditional list of deadly sins is still relevant for us today. If we are self-conscious about how it has been used to distort the truth and to victimize individuals, especially women, I believe it can still play a significantly positive role in the accurate diagnosis of our moral and spiritual condition. One major purpose of the book is to demonstrate the diagnostic uses of the traditional list of deadly sins.

But diagnosis is only half the battle. Once our condition is diagnosed, we seek the resources to cure us. The whole point of the book is that the deadly sins can be overcome, not through some miracle cure (such as a sudden conversion experience) but through the cultivation of virtues. There are various traditional lists of the virtues, including the list that combines Aristotle's four cardinal or natural virtues (justice, prudence, temperance, and fortitude) with Paul's three theological virtues (faith, hope, and love). The list offered by Chaucer in "The Parson's Tale" is especially interesting because it is set directly against the seven deadly sins and is meant to demonstrate that for each deadly sin there is at least one virtue that counteracts it.

But as I have already indicated, I will be using Erik Erikson's list of virtues because these virtues are presented in developmental sequence and thus relate to the various stages of the life cycle. His list includes hope, will, purpose, competence, fidelity, love, care, and wisdom. These virtues are "natural" in the sense that they are inherent strengths that all humans potentially possess. They are not accessible only to a few, to a moral or spiritual elite. But they are also "God-given," because they are part of a preestablished ground plan, appearing at their appointed time through no human design or effort. We do not create virtues; they are created in and for us. But we can cultivate them and help them become a more effective force in our lives. I call them the saving virtues because they are able so to energize our lives that the deadly sins lose their effective power over us.

CHAPTER TWO

The Sins of Infancy and Early Childhood

More than thirty-five years ago, Erik Erikson suggested that each individual goes through eight stages in life.[1] In each stage, we experience a crisis that is crucial for our continued development. The following schedule indicates the crisis or conflict situation for each of the eight stages:

Stage	Age	Crisis
Infancy	0 – 1	Basic trust v. basic mistrust
Early childhood	1 – 3	Autonomy v. shame and doubt
Play age	3 – 5	Initiative v. guilt
School age	5 – 12	Industry v. inferiority
Adolescence	12 – 18	Identity v. identity confusion
Young adulthood	18 – 40	Intimacy v. isolation
Adulthood	40 – 65	Generativity v. stagnation
Mature adulthood	65 +	Integrity v. despair

Erikson says that the ideal working-through of each crisis is not to eliminate the "negative" pole (mistrust, shame, doubt, guilt, and so on). Instead, successful resolution of the crisis is a matter of finding an appropriate ratio between the positive and negative poles. For healthy growth, the positive pole needs to predominate, but not so much that there is no place for the negative. It is appropriate for an individual to have some mistrust (since the world is not totally trustworthy), to have some degree of shame (otherwise one is shameless), to experience guilt (otherwise one lacks conscience), and so forth.

Space does not allow us to provide a detailed summary of Erikson's life-cycle theory. I have provided this in my book, *Life Cycle Theory and Pastoral Care*.[2] Nor is it possible to consider recent criticisms of Erikson's life-cycle theory, including the criticism that the crises for the earlier stages reflect male rather than female experience.[3] This criticism is an important one, and it should on some occasion be addressed directly, since it has implications for Erikson's own religious vision. In the meantime, I view the present book as an initial step toward a more systematic discussion of Erikson's life-cycle theory vis-à-vis recent criticisms.

My basic proposal is that there is a deadly sin for each life-cycle stage. Since Erikson's theory includes eight stages, I propose going back to the earliest lists of deadly sins, when there were eight, not seven, sins. By linking the deadly sins to Erikson's life-cycle stages, I am suggesting that the deadly sins are directly involved in the developmental process.

This is not an entirely novel approach. In *From Sin to Wholeness*, Brian W. Grant has proposed that the seven deadly sins are related to three developmental periods in life.[4] The sins of a "falsely extended childhood" are sloth and gluttony; the sins of "misplaced adolescence" are anger and lust; and the sins of "exaggerated adulthood" are greed, envy, and pride. For Grant, these sins are not limited to the period in which they emerge: adults are certainly capable of all seven sins, and the adult sins are often found among children and adolescents. Instead his point is that each sin reflects the distortion of a "good aim" typically found in the period of life to which it has been assigned. Grant emphasizes that sin involves "missing the mark." It is the result of a good aim that went awry.

My proposal is based on a closer linkage of the traditional lists of sins and Erikson's life-cycle stages. I suggest that there is a deadly sin for each stage. Each sin is appropriate to the stage to which it is assigned, and is a prominent factor in our moral and spiritual life during that period. It is appropriate and prominent because it reflects the basic psychodynamics of the stage in question, developing out of the dynamics of that stage. But once the sin has emerged and has gained center stage for a season, it does not disappear. Instead it becomes a permanent part of our total sin repertoire. Conversely, a sin whose normal time of ascendancy has not yet arrived may appear at an earlier stage. For example, a child's behavior may reflect a deadly sin that has been ascribed to an adult stage of life, and this sin may team up with the sin appropriate to the child's stage of life. The combination of sins can have an especially demoralizing effect on the child. Thus, the sins are not rigidly tied to the stage assigned but are linked to the stages through their common psychodynamics. This means that the sins are not just behaviors but dispositions dynamically rooted in the personality. The sin is assigned to a particular stage on the grounds that it is dynamically related to the central crisis of that stage.

To provide a deadly sin for each of the eight stages, I have reinstated melancholy to the list. Gregory the Great subsumed apathy under melancholy. Another early church theologian, Alcuin, subsumed melancholy under apathy. Alcuin's proposal prevailed, and apathy was accepted as the name for the combined sin, which then in the English language became sloth. Although apathy may retain elements of melancholy, it is doubtful that sloth has any melancholic connotation. So when sloth became the name for this sin, all traces of the sin of melancholy disappeared. Consequently, I propose that we restore melancholy to the list, as the eighth deadly sin, and call the seventh sin apathy instead of sloth.

Restoring one of the original sins to the list is preferable to introducing an entirely new sin. For on what grounds would we choose a new sin to add to the list? In his book *Conquering the Seven Deadly Sins*, Lance Webb adds a chapter on "Anxiety and Worry" to chapters on the traditional seven deadly sins.[5] Anxiety and worry can be serious sins, but we could just as easily propose other sins, like cruelty, deception, and forgetting.[6] To avoid arbitrariness, it seems best to restore one of the sins that was dropped from the original lists.

In addition, I propose to speak of apathy instead of sloth, because this is a more accurate rendering of the Latin word *acedia*. Though Chaucer views the two words as nearly synonymous, saying that *acedia* "is the rotten-hearted sin of Sloth," the word "sloth" has now come to mean laziness, which is not at all what *acedia* originally meant. On the other hand, "apathy" does not capture all of the meaning of *acedia*, because acedia also includes indifference. So I will make reference to indifference as well when I discuss the sin of apathy.

My proposed linkage of deadly sins and life-cycle stages is displayed in table 1. The basic rationale for the linkage is that the sin assigned to a given stage grows out of the dynamics of that stage. As dispositional and not merely behavioral, the sin is a negative capacity or potential that develops out of the crisis situation of the stage to which it has been assigned. Other sins not included in the traditional list may certainly emerge from these same dynamics, but we would then view them as "branches" of the deadly sin. Furthermore, the deadly sins are not merely the outgrowth of the negative pole of a given stage, be-

TABLE 1: ERIKSON'S LIFE-CYCLE STAGES AND THE DEADLY SINS

Mature adulthood	Melancholy							
Adulthood		Apathy						
Young adulthood			Lust					
Adolescence				Pride				
School age					Envy			
Play age						Greed		
Early childhood							Anger	
Infancy								Gluttony

cause the deadly sin may also develop from an excess of the positive. In any case, the sin is rooted in the complex interrelationship of the positive and negative poles.

The linkages between deadly sins and life-cycle stages cannot merely be asserted. They have to be demonstrated. I will therefore discuss the first two of the linkages in this chapter, and follow with two additional linkages in each of the three succeeding chapters.

Infancy and the Deadly Sin of Gluttony

For Erikson, the infant's first crisis centers on trust and mistrust. Dependent on other people for life's basic needs, the infant is placed in a situation where trust is all-important. If those who provide for us are basically reliable, trust will begin to develop. But those are the same people who are also most likely to evoke mistrust. As trustworthy, they raise expectations of continued care. When they fail to meet these expectations, we feel betrayed and abandoned, and in such perceived betrayal the seeds of mistrust are sown. Obviously those who care for us cannot meet our needs with perfect consistency. Even if they could, they would not be doing us a favor in the long run, for they might create the false impression that the world exists only to respond to our needs. So mistrust is inevitable, and this produces a conflict between basic trust and basic mistrust.

In infancy we also develop a rudimentary level of self-trust. In the early months of life, we have hostile urges, such as the impulse to bite and hit, that may cause the caring person to withdraw or withhold sustenance. Sensing that the consequences of such behavior are the loss of food, comfort, and pleasurable attention, we seek to control our hostile urges, and out of such efforts, rudimentary as they may be, a sense of self-trust begins to emerge. So the basic trust that develops in this stage involves a fundamental trust in others and in ourselves. In the first case, the trust is rooted in our confidence that the others have things under control. In the latter case, it is rooted in our confidence that we can exercise some control over ourselves.

I have assigned gluttony to the first stage of life. What is gluttony? Basically it is an excessive, seemingly insatiable desire for food and drink. To be a glutton is to want more food or drink than is needed, and to want it now, not some time in the future. Strictly speaking, gluttony concerns food and drink, but it has also been understood metaphorically, as when we say that someone with an excessive capacity to endure abuse is a glutton for punishment. What makes gluttony sinful?

Its sinfulness lies not simply in the excessive eating or drinking but in the attitudes or dispositions that lie behind this behavior. Basically, gluttony reflects a careless attitude toward life and beauty. As a careless attitude toward *life*, it can result in severe physical and emotional impairment and can even cause death. We recognize how much it threatens life when we say, "If I eat any more, I'll simply burst." Thus gluttony is the abuse of what is essential to our survival, whether this involves abuse of substances we absorb into our bodies or abuse of the body itself. As a careless attitude toward *beauty*, gluttony does not find pleasure in the taste of food and drink but cares only about the amount of it. That reflects a lack of aesthetic appreciation for the created world: "Gluttony does not give a particular value to anything it consumes. It does not savor. It only devours."[7]

Gluttony also reflects a destructive attitude toward companionship. The gluttonous are persons "who remove themselves from any caring for others, even from their companions at the moment." They also "remove themselves from the concern that others feel for them."[8] In this regard, many writers on the deadly sin of gluttony consider alcoholism and drug abuse to be particularly destructive forms of gluttony. They follow Chaucer, whose parson says, "Gluttony is an immeasurable appetite to eat or drink. Drunkenness is the horrible sepulchre of man's reason." And Kenneth Slack notes that drug addiction has proved so "appallingly dangerous as to give macabre accuracy to the word 'deadly.'"[9]

On the other hand, Stanford Lyman suggests that some forms of gluttony may promote social good. The glutton for work may, by example, enable others to increase their own capacity for productive work. The narrowly focused intellectual work of the glutton for knowledge, the so-called bookworm, may prove more valuable to society than the contributions of the well-rounded student. The glutton for punishment, or masochist, is valuable in situations that require the endurance of unusual amounts of physical or mental pain.

Still, in general, gluttony reflects a careless attitude toward life and beauty and a destructive attitude toward companionship. Since these are the attitudes that fuel gluttony, I suggest that gluttony is rooted dynamically in the infancy stage of the life cycle, reflecting the conflict of trust versus mistrust. The careless and destructive attitudes of gluttony reveal either a deep mistrust or an excessive degree of trust. The mistrustful side of gluttony involves a fear of future deprivation. The fear arises when we discover that we cannot trust the persons who are responsible for our well-being to meet needs as they arise. We are hungry, but no food is offered. We require love and affection, but they are withheld. Faced with an uncertain situation, we try to get more than enough now in order to make provision for those times in the future when real needs are not met. From the desire to get more than enough now, gluttony is born. It often becomes a vicious cycle, for when we anticipate future deprivation we become overly demanding in the present, and this demandingness prompts our caretakers to limit the supply of goods for fear that we will become "spoiled." Our demands for physical nurturance, love, and affection can destroy the very companionship we need to sustain our trust in the world and in ourselves.

Another side of gluttony is an excessive or indiscriminate trust. In the first months of life, we discover that the world is filled with objects that can make us happy and contented. We begin to associate happiness and well-being with the substances we take into our bodies. But not all substances in the outside world have "good" effects when they are taken in. As we gain more experience with taking things in, we learn to discriminate between good and bad substances. Parents help us to do this by warning, "Don't put that in your mouth. It's not good for you." We also learn to make our own judgments as to what are good and bad substances, usually doing so on the basis of taste. Parents often attempt to overrule such judgments: "Maybe it tastes bad, but it's good for you." By making such judgments, even if they are challenged by our parents, we develop the art of discrimination, and this is the important thing, since the glutton lacks taste, taking in anything and everything indiscriminately.

Thus gluttony reflects indiscriminate trust. It has the attitude "I can take this into my body, and it will not hurt me." Yes, the world has some wonderful life-sustaining and pleasure-sustaining substances. But it also has substances that are dangerous. Some substances are safe in small doses but dangerous in larger doses. Some are dangerous regardless of the amount taken in. Some are immediately life-threatening. Others destroy the body a little at a time, as agents of a slow death. The task of becoming discriminating about such substances begins in infancy. Our natural tendency to trust needs to be refined and made more discriminating, because the world is not entirely trustworthy. This means that there is need for healthy mistrust, and therefore for discriminating as opposed to indiscriminate trust. The infant who is indiscriminately trustful reveals a love of life and appreciation for the pleasures the world affords. But the child and adult who persist in this indiscriminate trust become careless of life (reckless) and unappreciative of the world's beauty (tasteless). Then they are enslaved by the deadly sin of gluttony.

As a deadly sin, gluttony may be found among people of all ages. But in developmental terms, it is the first sin. Many people argue that pride is the first sin, the chief of sins. Maybe this can be argued for on theological grounds. But developmentally our first sin is not pride but gluttony. Gluttony is the sin of mistrust and indiscriminate trust.

Early Childhood and the Deadly Sin of Anger

In one of his descriptions of the second stage of the life cycle, Erikson refers to Benjamin Spock's book on childrearing. Under the headings of "The One-Year-Old" and "Managing Young Children," Spock discusses such topics as feeling one's oats, the passion to explore, getting more dependent and independent at the same time, the control of aggression, anger as a normal feeling at this age, and temper tantrums.[10] In their book on childrearing, Ilg and Ames describe the years between ages one and three as fairly turbulent: "Eighteen months is not one of the 'better' ages if we measure goodness in terms of minding, responding to commands, keeping within reasonable limits." Two years of age provides a "breathing space for child as well as mother," but two-and-a-half "is a peak age of disequilibrium. It is an 'age of violent emotions.'"[11] No wonder that Erikson concludes that this developmental stage "portrays sinister forces which are leashed and unleashed, especially in the guerrilla warfare of unequal wills; for the child is often unequal to his own violent drives, and parent and child unequal to each other."[12]

This period is a crisis involving autonomy, on the one hand, and our susceptibility to shame and doubt, on the other. The autonomy we seek is the simple recognition of the fact that we have a right to have a will of our own. We want to "do it myself" and insist that others "can't make me do it." Our new bid for autonomy is made possible by our capacity to control arm, hand, and sphincter muscles. With that capacity we can "hold on" and "let go" at will—grasping, dropping, and throwing things, clinging to objects one moment and discarding them the next. We use our abilities to hold on and let go in a battle against our parents who, prior to this stage, had all the power to themselves. As Ilg and Ames point out, the "18-monther walks down a one-way street . . . and this street more often than not seems to lead in a direction exactly opposite to that which the adult has in mind. Asked to 'come here, dear,' he either stands still or runs in the opposite direction. . . . Ask him to put something in the wastebasket, and he is more likely to empty out what is already in it. Hold out your hand for the cup he has just drained, he will drop it onto the floor."[13] The child's attitudes illustrate what Erikson calls the "enormous value with which the still highly dependent child begins to endow his autonomous will."[14]

These illustrations make autonomy seem unattractive, as though it means being stubborn and resistant. Yet it is the *positive* pole of this stage's conflict. Why? Because the battle for autonomy, with its clash of wills, eventually evolves into a more secure autonomy reflecting a sense of self-control, appropriate self-esteem, and personal dignity. When this genuine expression of autonomy replaces the more aggressive and erratic form, there is a less rigid and uncompromising insistence on having our own way, less emotional anarchy, and less irrational fear of being controlled by others and being out of control ourselves. A good sign that such autonomy is beginning to form is our ability to hold on and let go in a more relaxed fashion: "'To hold' can become a destructive and cruel retaining or restraining, or it can become a pattern of care: 'to have and to hold.'" To let go can be the "letting loose" of destructive forces, or it can become a relaxed "letting pass" and "letting be." Genuine autonomy occurs when we have become relaxed about the assertion of our will. We do not allow our will to be subdued or broken, but at the same time we do not always insist on having our way.

The negative pole of this stage is shame and doubt. Shame is a major factor because our muscle system is beginning to develop and we are learning to coordinate a number of highly conflicting action patterns. As we develop our ability to walk, to control our bowels, to hold a glass or silverware, we are very conscious of being the object of attention, and we feel self-conscious. Our failure to perform our tasks successfully can be embarrassing, humiliating, and shame producing. We try to walk across the room but fail. Shame results and we feel exposed. As Erikson puts it, "Shame is early expressed in an impulse to bury one's face, or to sink, right then and there, into the ground." He warns that parents often exploit our sensitivity to being exposed in this way by shaming us into obedience and compliance with their demands. The problem is that shaming "does not result in a sense of propriety but in a secret determination to try to get away with things unseen, if, indeed, it does not result in deliberate shamelessness."[15]

Erikson says that "doubt is the brother of shame."[16] The same experiences of failure that lead to shame may also lead to doubt. Such episodes also threaten the trust established in infancy, as we find the world is less supportive than we imagined. We also discover that our bodies are not to be trusted because they fail to perform as we want them to. This creates doubt toward the world and ourselves, and we respond by attempting to change what we have the power to change, ourselves. Unfortunately, self-control growing out of doubt instead of autonomy becomes self-manipulative. Doubt is overcome, but only because we now encounter the world through repetitive and thus highly predictable actions. We become obsessive and compulsive.

Anger is the deadly sin that arises in this stage of the life cycle. It is dynamically rooted in the conflict of autonomy versus shame and doubt. Anger is a feeling that may result from injury, mistreatment, or opposition. It usually shows itself in a desire to hit out at someone or something. "Anger" is the broadest term for emotional agitation aroused by great displeasure. Related words specify the intensity or duration of the emotional agitation. Thus, rage is a violent outburst of anger in which self-control is lost, and fury is an overwhelming rage of such frenzy that it borders on madness. There are also related words that indicate instances where anger has some real justification. Thus indignation is righteous anger aroused by what is considered unjust, and wrath is deep indignation that expresses itself in a desire to punish or get revenge. The fact that one form of anger is indignation proves that anger is not a sin in every instance.

What then makes it a sin? In "The Parson's Tale," Chaucer says that "anger against wickedness, where there is wrath without bitterness, is good, but anger that seeks vengeance is wicked." This means that indignation is good but wrath is sinful. The parson has nothing to say about rage and fury, probably because these concern only the intensity and duration of anger, not the attitude behind it. Henry Fairlie, in his book on the deadly sins, makes a similar point. He says that what makes anger a deadly sin is our determination to take vengeance against the person or persons who made us angry.

But Lyman challenges the view that the basic issue is vengeance. He believes that anger is most deadly when it is self-destructive. To him, anger is the "aggressive defense of an injured self," and it takes a variety of forms. In the very young child, it is a response to punishment and only under the most extreme provocations does it issue in rage. Later, when we are punished for actions we did not know were prohibited, we become resentful and an internalized rage develops. But the deepest anger of all, according to Lyman, occurs when we are punished for good and lovable deeds. Then we experience a deep psychic hurt, a wound to the very core of our self-esteem, and we respond with an "openly hostile attitude wherever sympathetic response is offered." Thus, what makes anger a deadly sin is the barrier it erects, making it impossible for us to be loved by another. What makes it a deadly sin is not its insistence on taking revenge but its rejection of the genuine efforts of other persons to offer support and love. Such rejection of others is based ultimately on self-rejection, the loss of self-esteem.[17]

As we have seen, Spock and other experts view the early childhood stage as one of aggression and violent emotions. It makes sense, then, to say that the attitude of anger emerges in this stage of development. In fact, as Spock makes clear, anger is a "normal emotion" during early childhood. But that it is normal does not mean that it is not sinful. Shame and doubt are the outward manifestations of anger that cuts us off from those who want to offer support and love. Genuine autonomy reflects a basic faith in ourselves and others and leads us to open ourselves to such offers. Shame and doubt undermine that faith and cause us to erect barriers to keep others away. The experience of shame and doubt is inevitable in early childhood. But when such experiences are counterbalanced by experiences of real autonomy, we are able to endure the shame of exposure and are not compelled to hide from others. Nor do we need to overcome our doubts by carefully staging all our encounters in the world, making them predictable and therefore totally meaningless. The effort to wall ourselves off from others is an expression of deep anger, whether it issues in overt acts of defiance and revenge, or is turned inward in the form of silent rage.

In short, anger is a sin when it leads to erecting barriers between ourselves and others. And shame, doubt, and false autonomy are the experiences of early childhood that cause us to become angry. But not all anger is sinful. Anger becomes a deadly sin when it cuts us off from others, especially from those who want to express their love and support. The desire for revenge may reflect an unhealthy and even sinful attitude in a small child. It reveals the wish to hurt another person, whether or not the child has the power to do so. But the really deadly form of anger is its self-destructiveness, as reflected in our rejection of love. Such rejection is usually caused when a parent rejects the child's own expressions of love, affection, and kindness. That means that parents are often the precipitators of the child's deadly sin of anger. Yet it is the child in whom the deadly attitude takes form who becomes the ultimate victim of the sin of anger.

The Dispositional Roots of
Gluttony and Anger

The sins of gluttony and anger are grounded in the root sins identified in chapter 1: rebellion, personal bondage, and isolation or estrangement. Take gluttony. When gluttony involves indiscriminate trust, it becomes a form of *personal bondage* as we become controlled by substances that are not good for us. When it involves fear of future deprivation, its determination to get more than is needed now results from a perceived absence of support and nurturance, and thus from a profound sense of *isolation* from those on whom we are deeply dependent. Gluttony may also reflect *rebellion* as it engages in a fruitless and self-destructive battle against the inherent limitations of the body.

Anger too is grounded in all three root sins. It has an element of *rebellion*, the refusal to accept the authority of another person (usually a parent). But through the centuries, Christians have focused so much on the rebellion theme—the child's refusal to do what parents expect or demand—that they have tended to neglect the themes of personal bondage and isolation. Behaviorally, anger often takes the form of rebellion. But, attitudinally or dispositionally, it arises out of personal bondage and leads to isolation from others. Anger is produced by experiences of personal failure and humiliation or the inability to evoke positive acclaim and assurances from persons who have considerable influence on how we perceive ourselves. Thus it has roots in *personal bondage*. The result is anger that becomes internalized rage against the assaults on our self-image. If the bondage is not overcome through offsetting experiences of genuine autonomy which enable us to acquire a sense of self-control, appropriate self-esteem, and personal dignity in spite of these assaults, the anger will reflect the third root sin, *isolation*. Now we no longer try to relate to others, since they are perceived as persons who only judge and curse us. When this happens, our anger becomes a vicious circle, leading us to avoid those contacts with other persons which are essential to our release from personal bondage.

CHAPTER THREE

The Sins of the Play Age
and School Age

The next two sins on our list—greed and envy—reflect the dynamics
of the play age (third stage of the life cycle) and school age (fourth
stage). Greed is linked to the crisis of initiative versus guilt, which occurs between ages three and five, and envy is linked to the crisis of industry versus inferiority, which occurs between ages five and twelve.
Of course, these sins, like those discussed in the previous chapter, are
found among persons who are older than this and perhaps among children who are younger. But the sins are closely associated with the dynamics of these two stages. Even among adults, greed and envy remain
linked to these dynamics as the dynamics continue to shape the lives
of individuals long after their time of developmental centrality has
passed.

The Play Age and the Deadly Sin of Greed

William James has said, "I am what I attend to." Children in the third
stage of the life cycle are capable of attending to virtually everything
that is going on around them. They are able to move independently
and vigorously. They are also intrusive, intruding into other bodies
through physical attack, into other ears and minds by aggressive talking, into space by vigorous locomotion, and into the unknown by consuming curiosity. Three new abilities support this stage, while also
bringing about its crisis:

1. We learn to move around more freely, even violently, and therefore establish a wider and seemingly unlimited radius of goals.

2. Our language develops to the point where we understand and can ask incessantly about innumerable things, often hearing just enough to misunderstand them thoroughly.

3. Both language and locomotion permit an expansion of imagination to so many roles that we cannot avoid frightening ourselves with what we ourselves have dreamed and thought up.

Out of these developments, a sense of initiative emerges, which serves as the basis for a realistic sense of ambition and purpose. Initiative, the positive pole of this stage, means the capacity not only to do things but to do them with vitality. When our intrusiveness is being transformed into genuine initiative, we are in the free possession of a certain surplus of energy that permits us "to forget many failures rather quickly and to approach new areas that seem desirable, even if they also seem dangerous, with undiminished zest and some increased sense of direction."[1]

Initiative also involves a capacity to cooperate with others: "At no time is the individual more ready to learn quickly and avidly, to become big in the sense of sharing obligation, discipline, and performance rather than power, in the sense of *making things instead of 'making' people*, than during this period of his development. He is also eager and able to *make things together*, to combine with other children for the purpose of constructing and planning, instead of trying to boss and coerce them."[2] Thus initiative involves cooperative enterprise, a shift from attacking persons to attacking a project—and doing so in concert with other children.

The negative pole of this stage is guilt. Guilt is the unavoidable result of the developments occurring in the play age. Our ability to move around freely gives us a wider and seemingly unlimited radius of goals, but it also produces guilt when we transgress established boundaries. The unlimited radius of goals is only apparent, for there are goals that are definitely forbidden or "out of bounds." The acquisition of language also opens a whole new world to us but one that is potentially guilt producing. Some language—"dirty words"—is always out of bounds. Other language meets with approval in some circumstances and disapproval in others ("What you say is true, but, please, not a word of it when your father is around"). Our imagination is greatly expanded in this period, and that too is potentially cause for guilt as we fantasize ourselves in forbidden roles and situations. The imagination is a world of secret thoughts and images, and we become afraid that the secret thoughts will be found out. A conscience develops as the child "now hears, as it were, God's voice without seeing

God" and "begins automatically to feel guilty even for mere thoughts and for deeds which nobody has watched."[3]

The development of conscience is essential to genuine morality, but the conscience of the child at this stage *can* be primitive, cruel and uncompromising, as may be observed in instances where children learn to constrict themselves to the point of over-all inhibition."[4] In contrast, a *good* conscience forms when we gradually develop a sense of responsibility reflected, first, in a simple feeling for the institutions, functions, and values that permit us to anticipate our responsible participation as an adult, and second, in a growing concern to take care of ourselves and younger children. Adults can help in the development of this good conscience by challenging through their example the child's suspicion that the whole matter of obedience is one of arbitrary power, not mutual goodness. Children of this age often develop deep resentments toward parents who do not appear to live up to the conscience they have fostered in the child. For children who come to believe that parental authority is based on the parent's superior power rather than moral example, "morality can become synonymous with vindictiveness and with the suppression of others."[5]

I have assigned greed to this stage. Greed or greediness implies an insatiable desire to possess or acquire something in an amount that is far greater than we need. More specific forms of greed include (1) avariciousness, which stresses greed for money or riches, and often implies miserliness; (2) acquisitiveness, which suggests an excessive effort in acquiring or accumulating wealth or material possessions; and (3) covetousness, which implies greed for something that another person rightfully possesses.

Chaucer's parson describes greed or avarice as a "lecherous desire for earthly things, a kind of idolatry." On the other hand, Henry Fairlie, in his book on the deadly sins, contends that greed is "not so much the love of possessions, as the love merely of possessing." It is the "love of possessing for its own sake."[6] Yet both agree that greed involves an inordinate or insatiable desire that knows no bounds. Where gluttony tests the limits of the body until it can take no more, greed tests and often exceeds the limits of social and legal propriety to see what it can "get away with."

But perhaps the most suggestive relationship between greed and other deadly sins is between greed, envy, and pride. As Stanford Lyman points out, greed often results from our envy of the better-off and from a certain self-pride, which then propel the acquisitive action necessary to remove inequalities and restore or raise dignity. The problem, though, is that greed has a tendency to become independent of its origins and forgets that its initial purpose was to right the wrongs of inequality: "The inequalities that breed envious competition, also engender a permanent restlessness, characterized on the one hand by the insatiable desire to acquire more and more and on the other by a miserable but nagging apprehension that whatever one has or gets is not and never can be enough."[7] Thus, the problem with greed is that it knows no limits; it does not know when enough is enough.

What makes greed a deadly sin? Greed is deadly because it distracts us from what is important in life. Thus Fairlie notes that the "pursuit of wealth and possessions, when conducted with such singlemindedness as it is in our societies, constantly distracts us from spiritual things and not the least from the spiritual side of our natures."[8] Furthermore, greed is deadly because it distorts our vision and gives us a false perception of ourselves and the world. Thus Kenneth Slack points out that in Jesus' parable of the rich fool the problem is not that the man acquired his possessions unfairly, dishonestly, or even by hard dealing. We are not necessarily to assume that he was avaricious or covetous. The real issue is what conclusions he drew once he had acquired his possessions. He thought he was protected from every contingency of life. But he was sadly mistaken. He misperceived his real situation. What he had not planned for, could not plan for, was the fact that this night his life would end. Thus the parable relates how greed, as acquisitiveness, leads to a distorted perception of ourselves and our situation in the world.

Slack also points out that greed caused the "total atrophying" of the rich fool's imagination. He was unable to think of anything to do with the unexpected bumper crops except to build bigger barns to hold them, and to provide security for himself. His inability to perceive his true situation was partly due to the atrophying of his imagination. He became cautious and self-protective and was unable to give thought to how his great possessions might be used to improve the lives of other persons.[9]

Thus greed is a deadly sin because it leads to a distorted view of reality and a narrowing of vision and imagination. Lyman points to such distortion in popular delusions of instant wealth, including the South Sea Bubble, the Gold Rush, and, we might add, lotteries and sweepstakes. He observes the atrophying of imagination in the case of white-collar crime. Imaginative use of material resources for good is replaced with self-serving plots. And when the plots are discovered, there are denials of wrongdoing. Stock swindlers deny that they actually injured anyone, or if they admit the injury, they claim that their victims deserved what they got, because they allowed their own greed to overwhelm their better judgment.[10] What atrophies here is the moral imagination so crucial to an active conscience.

How does the deadly sin of greed relate to the third stage of the life cycle? Obviously, if we view greed only in terms of avarice, the insatiable desire for money or riches, it would not make sense to locate greed in the third stage. Children between the ages of three and five may have some rudimentary appreciation for the value of money, but they are certainly not consumed with a desire for it. But if we are concerned with the personal dispositions that give rise to greed, the dynamics of this stage are certainly relevant. The first of the three developments in this stage is our ability to envision a wider and seemingly unlimited radius of goals. This introduces the necessary conditions for the insatiable desire associated with greed. From the sense of the seemingly unlimited radius of goals, we may gain the false impression that there is no limit to what we may desire to do or to have. The same can be said of the child's intrusiveness. Two aspects of this are especially relevant to greed. One is the tendency toward excess—too much talk, too vigorous locomotion, too much curiosity. Such excess is the very heart of greed, which also knows no limits. Another aspect is the tendency to deny the rights and privileges of others. Others' possessions are handled and often mishandled. Their quiet time is invaded by loud talk. Their privacy is invaded through vigorous locomotion and consuming curiosity. Such disregard for the property and rights of others is a common feature of greed, where our insatiable desire seems to justify a disregard for others.

Though initiative refines intrusiveness, it does not inhibit it altogether. Initiative is based on a "realistic sense of ambition and purpose." In contrast, greed involves an unrealistic sense of ambition and purpose. Greed is ambition and purpose that have no limits, that follow no commonly agreed upon rules or guidelines. Initiative also refines the imagination so that it gets directed toward realistic planning and goals. Initiative means envisioning outcomes that are within the realm of possibility, whereas greed is based on unrealistic imaginings, on illusions and delusions. Erikson calls this stage the play age because this is when we discover that play allows us to try out roles, to develop plans and construct scenes, and to rehearse the future. As one form of imagination, play transforms greed into initiative. That is especially evident in cooperative play, where arguments over possessions ("That's mine, you can't have it") give way to collaborative enterprise

("That's interesting. May I see how it works?"). Thus greed is re-strained or channeled through initiative. Because greed feeds and is fed by intrusiveness, any rechanneling of intrusiveness into initiative strikes a blow against greed.

Greed is also linked dynamically to guilt, the negative pole of this life-cycle stage. Greed is not the only reason for guilt's emerging at this stage, but the characteristics of greed dovetail very nicely with the form of guilt that emerges. Greed reflects the guilt of trespassing or transgressing, the failure to respect social boundaries in the head-long pursuit of our desires and aims. In addition, greed reflects the guilt of excess, or of the insatiable desire for more of whatever is val-ued, whether we have any right to it or not. Erikson's descriptions of the intrusiveness of children capture both features of guilt. The intru-sive child ignores boundaries and limits and does everything to excess (too much talk, too loud, too aggressive). And this is precisely how greed functions. It too ignores boundaries, and it too does everything to excess. The task set before those who are responsible for the moral and spiritual formation of the child is to help transform intrusiveness into initiative by curbing and regulating the transgressions and ex-cesses without inhibiting genuine desire.

Intrusiveness is also likely to produce distortion. Intrusive children are largely unaware of the influence their behavior is having on the environment around them. The intrusive child does not perceive the external world accurately or perceptively. The world appears boun-daryless, but it is not. It appears that we may take possession of any-thing in this world that appeals to us, that evokes our desire; but this is not the case. Many things already belong to someone else. In contrast to intrusive children, children who become genuine initiators are tak-ing the environment itself into consideration and are adapting their behavior to the environment in a reality-testing way. Thus here again greed and intrusiveness go hand in hand, for all forms of intrusive be-havior distort the external world in the same manner that greed dis-torts it.

In light of the distortion that greed produces, this deadly sin draws our attention to the problem of appearance and reality. And that is precisely what the third stage of the life cycle, with its emphasis on dreams, fantasy, and play, is all about. True imagination, which devel-ops in this stage, takes the world's boundaries into account (whether the boundaries are physical or moral) and is able to test the bound-aries with considerable realism because it does not ignore or disre-gard them. For greed such boundaries are either nonexistent ("I go wherever my desires take me") or they are that solid, impregnable wall that suddenly appears out of nowhere ("This night, your life is required of you").

In short, the third stage of the life cycle sows the seeds of greed. But it also sows the seeds of responsibility, reflected in an emerging respect for the functions and roles represented by responsible adults, who gain this respect through moral example, not arbitrary power; in the eager assumption of obligations, simple and routinized as they may be; and in a concern to take care of oneself and others, such as younger siblings. Children and adults of good conscience are not inhibited, unable to act on their desires. But neither are they overwhelmed by insatiable desire. Their desires are instead in the process of being refined by a disposition of responsible caring, both toward themselves and toward others. Persons of good conscience have a concern for the welfare of the natural world as well, perceiving that it is not there for the taking but is there for mutual enrichment. In contrast, the attitude of greed toward the social and natural world is fundamentally irresponsible and careless.

The School Age and the Deadly Sin of Envy

Though all children need to play, they sooner or later become dissatisfied with "mere" playing. They also want a sense of being useful. Erikson makes this point in his description of the fourth stage of the life cycle, the school age, which involves the crisis of industry and inferiority. At this age, we feel exploited or patronized if we are not allowed or encouraged to develop a sense of industry. Such industry involves adjustment to the laws of the tool world and becoming an eager participant in a productive situation. It means sublimating personal disappointments in the interest of this productive aim, and it means taking pleasure in the completion of projects through steady attention and perseverance.[11]

In the previous stage, there was a swing from an inner upheaval to a new mastery (i.e., from pure intrusiveness to channeled initiative) and radically new developments in physical maturation (i.e., vigorous locomotion and the capacity to talk freely). There is nothing quite like this in the school age. There are no radically new developments in physical maturation that force us to change our whole approach to the world around us. Still, this stage is socially decisive, because it provides a lasting basis for cooperative participation in productive adult life. With the onset of the school age, we acquire our "first real sense of division of labor and of differential opportunity."[12]

The danger at this stage, and the major reason that this potentially calm period (from a physical standpoint) may be full of conflict, is the emergence of a sense of inferiority. Feelings of inferiority can have various causes. They may be due to an inadequate resolution of the conflicts of the preceding stage and reflect our desire to be the little child at home rather than the big child at school. They may be due to the fact that family life did not prepare us for school life. Or school life may fail to sustain the promises of earlier stages: what we learned to do well in the previous stage may not count for much with our teachers and classmates. Or the problem may be that we are potentially able to excel in ways that for the time being are dormant. But whatever the cause of our feelings of inferiority, we learn during the school age that we differ from our classmates in our abilities. None of us can escape at least a fleeting sense of inferiority in comparing our abilities with those of schoolmates. And sooner or later we all discover that we are unable to master some aspect of school life, whether a certain academic subject, athletic skill, or special interest.

Such experiences, if not too severe, may contribute to a sense of industry if we are able to sublimate our personal disappointment in pursuit of common goals and purposes. This is all part of being a "good citizen" and a "good sport." But there are more severe or chronic experiences of inferiority that are due to our general inability to do what is expected of us, to emotional problems generated by circumstances outside the school, to adjustment problems at school, or to various other causes. In such cases, our sense of inferiority is more pervasive, and it severely limits our ability to participate in productive activities. School-age children win recognition by producing things. Those who are unable to produce gain notoriety, not recognition, and this makes them feel even more inferior.

I have assigned the deadly sin of envy to the school-age stage of the life cycle. In its most basic meaning, envy is a feeling of discontent and ill will because of another person's advantages or possessions. It assumes that we keenly desire those advantages or possessions for ourselves. Chaucer's parson describes envy as "sorrow at the prosperity of others and joy in their hurt." Fairlie says that envy "must always try to level what it cannot emulate," and Slack notes that "envy is unusual in one significant respect in relation to the other six deadly sins. It is always directed at another person."[13] Greed is the desire for things, not persons. You can be lustful in your own imagination. You can be gluttonous by yourself. But envy is always directed against another person.

Envy is more than seeing that someone else has something that we want for ourselves. Envy forms when we believe that the other person's advantage or possession diminishes or brings disgrace on us. Once we believe that, we try to divest those we envy of their advantage, usually by trying to "pull the other person down" (e.g., by intimating to other interested parties that the envied person's advantage is spurious or ill gotten). Envy may also produce a psychological reaction of dejection or resentment that eventually results in apathy, one of the other deadly sins. Here the envious person sadly and grudgingly "accepts" the self-diminishment caused by the advantage of the envied person and is unable to do anything to change it.

Envy is not always a bad thing. There are times when it has positive effects. Envy is a resource for protesting the injustices of life. Children of the school age are confronted not only with the fact of differential ability but also with that of differential opportunity. Society has been so organized as to make it possible for some to benefit and others, equally deserving, to be deprived. Thus, as Lyman points out, when envy sparks the awareness that we are unfairly disadvantaged, it may be "transformed into an ideology of group righteousness" that in turn becomes the basis for social and political action. But Lyman also notes that "envy is more often experienced in isolation from one's associates, or as a secret sin to be hidden from view." When envy is privatized in this way, an individual may take revenge against particular persons who represent the advantaged group. Or if such revenge is impossible, envy becomes a smoldering resentment that is never appeased.[14] So one redeeming aspect of envy is that it can be the driving force behind a disadvantaged group's efforts to gain the benefits that other groups have. But such envy can also become privatized and degenerate into personal acts of revenge or develop into a lasting personal frustration.

Another positive effect of envy occurs when our awareness of another person's goods or qualities arouses in us the desire to acquire goods and qualities by meritorious effort. This is a benign form of envy because it does not direct any hostile attention toward the better-off. And because this form of envy is emulative rather than aggressive, it channels our resentments into legitimate activities. Rather than taking revenge against persons we envy, we emulate them. And, by emulating them, we hope to acquire in time the qualities they possess or the advantages they enjoy.

Envy is rooted in the dynamics of the stage of industry versus inferiority in the life cycle. It is rooted here since it reflects an actual or perceived inferiority to other persons. When we say, "I feel inferior," this is always in comparison with someone else whom we take to be superior. But the mere perception of inferiority to another is not itself envy. Envy is an attitude or disposition that develops out of the perception of inferiority, and that attitude may take many different forms. Actual or perceived inferiority may support an attempt to bring the envied person down to our own level. Or it may lead us to refuse to produce at the level at which we are capable. Erikson's theme of industry versus inferiority is mostly concerned with the second response, since it focuses on the person who feels inferior. Envy that does not attempt to cut another person down to size but instead gets internalized so that we avoid productive situations altogether is especially deadly. Then the effects of envy are immobilization and impotence. Remember the elder brother in Jesus' parable of the prodigal son. The advantages that the younger brother acquired on his return home produced in the elder brother an immobilizing envy. At the end of the story he was left standing outside the house, unable to act. And he was rendered impotent. Instead of adapting to or coping creatively with the situation in which he found himself, he was powerless. All he could do was to cite his past behavior: "Lo, I have been faithful these many years."

Envy that immobilizes and renders impotent is more subtly deadly than envy that takes revenge (e.g., Cain's revenge against Abel). It takes the envious person out of a productive situation, such as the process of reconciliation that the father in the parable initiated for the purpose of rehabilitating his younger son. When such envy prevails, a true sense of industry is impossible, because industry means being an eager participant in a productive situation and may well involve sublimating personal disappointments in the interest of the productive enterprise. The effect of an immobilizing envy is that we are unable to close the gap between our abilities and those of the person we envy, and even more tragically, we are unable to perform at levels of which we are fully capable ourselves.

The teacher's function during the school age is to motivate those who are less advantaged to work to their fullest potential. A related function is to help those who are advantaged to resist efforts of their envious peers to bring them down to their level. Some teachers also feel that it is necessary to offer those five-to-twelve-year-olds who are gifted warnings against the deadly sin of pride. But envy is more prevalent than pride in the school-age years, since children in the school age may still be unaware of their advantage or may sense that although they enjoy the advantage in one productive situation, they are the disadvantaged in others.

Erikson talks about the role the sublimation of our personal disappointments plays in the formation of a sense of industry. We might also say that the truly industrious have learned to sublimate their *envy*, making it work for rather than against them. Sublimation can occur through a shift from resentment to emulation. If another person is truly advantaged, possessing skills or abilities that we wish for ourselves, the other person may become a model for emulation. Of course, there is the danger of overidentification, of becoming someone's clone. Yet when emulation of another person enables us to acquire the same advantages, there is no further need to identify with that person. By being emulated, the envied person becomes the means for the envier's acquiring the same advantage. The father in the parable tried to assure his elder son that the brother's gain was not the elder son's loss. But the elder son was too much in the grip of envy to hear the assurances. His envy told him that his brother's advantage was his own disadvantage. The parable gives credibility to this perception, because it appears to suggest that the younger brother may be supplanting the elder brother in their father's affections. On the other hand, the younger brother has provided a model of action that his elder brother might have good reason to emulate. The younger brother's actions revealed that their father is a man who responds graciously to those who throw themselves on his mercy. Thus the envied one provided the envier with a model of action through which the envier might regain the status he has currently lost. Surely this is a better approach to the problem than Cain's decision to take revenge against his envied brother.

In advocating emulation as a way of dealing with envy, we ought not minimize the fact that some advantages enjoyed by others are unjust and unfair, or inaccessible, to those who do not enjoy them. There are clearly differential opportunities owing to injustices in the social system, and the school age is often the stage in life when individuals first discover that they are in fact the victims of social injustice. This is also the stage in life when we become acutely aware that others have natural abilities—"God-given talents"—that we do not have, and we discern that life itself gives some people an unfair advantage over others. Turning revenge into emulation and immobilizing resentment into engagement in a productive situation does not eliminate natural injustices. And where another person's advantages are gained through an unjust social system, it is difficult for the disadvantaged to imagine what they could possibly gain in moral or spiritual terms from emulating the advantaged. So emulation is not the answer for every case of envy. But my point is that it is generally better for the enviers themselves, especially when acting individually, to try to emulate instead of taking revenge against the person who is envied. I am also claiming that envy becomes deadly when it immobilizes us, causing us to avoid or withdraw from productive situations. When this happens, we become the victims of our own envy.

The Dispositional Roots of Greed and Envy

What are the roots of greed and envy? Do these sins reflect rebellion, personal bondage, or isolation? Greed reflects all three. Greed is a form of *rebellion*, because it ignores legitimate boundaries that have been established by society, and contingencies that are basic to human existence. But greed is also a sin of *isolation*. Hellbent on having what it wants and on having it now, greed pays little attention to companionship for its own sake. Friends are chosen because they have something of value that we covet, or because they are able to assist us in acquiring what we desire. Greedy persons are essentially asocial, viewing other persons as means to ends. Greed also produces *personal bondage*. The bondage that the greedy experience is the bondage of the imagination. Intending to possess the world's goods, the greedy are possessed by them. But even more, their preoccupation with possessing renders them less imaginative in relating to the world around them, and this is a form of personal bondage. Greed itself may know no bounds. But greed's effect is to blind our imaginations by limiting our imagination to the acquisitive realm of human life.

Envy too is rooted in all three sinful dispositions. With envy, there is usually a progression from rebellion to personal bondage to isolation. Thus, the first overt sign of envy is usually a rebellious attitude. When envious persons react against an injust situation involving differential opportunity, this is not the sin of rebellion. But when envy is so consuming or overwhelming that we find it impossible to participate in any productive situation whatsoever, this is a clear sign of *rebellion*. When teachers perceive that a child has become rebellious in this fashion, they seek ways to help the child engage in productive activity. Otherwise, the child may become permanently enslaved to envy.

Envy reflects *personal bondage*, because it immobilizes us and makes us impotent. Envious persons suffer under great self-imposed restrictions. If the greedy fail to recognize the real boundaries that exist in the real world, the envious are all too prone to erect self-imposed boundaries and limits, sometimes going so far as to convince themselves that these are boundaries in the real world that cannot be challenged or overcome.

The result of the immobilization and impotence of personal bondage is *isolation*, at least from situations having a productive purpose and from other persons engaged in those productive purposes. The envious person may enjoy the companionship of other envious persons who share a common dislike for those they envy. But envious persons who have become immobilized and are not using their envy constructively in the emulation of those they envy exclude themselves from productive living and from the companionship productive living can provide. Envious persons are not as lacking in companionship as the glutton, who eventually drives everyone away. But envious persons' companionship may be limited to nonproductive situations. The envious have little experience of the satisfaction that comes from working with others on a valued project. Nor do they experience the growth in personal character and emotional maturity that results from having to swallow personal disappointments in order to contribute to the larger aims of the productive group.

CHAPTER FOUR

The Sins of Adolescence
and Young Adulthood

The next two deadly sins on our list are pride and lust. In our schema, pride is dynamically rooted in the conflict of identity versus identity confusion, in adolescence. Lust is rooted in the conflict of intimacy versus isolation, of young adulthood. Again it must be emphasized that these deadly sins are not limited to their assigned stages in life. They are found among adults who are older, and perhaps among children who are younger. But they are rooted in the dynamics of the two stages, and they retain that dynamic core wherever they are found. As these dynamics continue to shape our lives in the later stages of the life cycle, pride and lust continue to have their influence.

Adolescence and the Deadly Sin of Pride

Erikson first used the term "identity crisis" while working in a veterans' rehabilitation clinic during World War II.[1] He used it to describe the situation of veterans who were neither shellshocked nor malingerers but who, through the exigencies of war, had "lost a sense of personal sameness and historical continuity." Later he observed the same emotional disturbances in "severely conflicted young people whose sense of confusion is due, rather, to a war within themselves." But the major development in his thinking about identity came when he began to recognize that what he had seen in the clinical setting was a "pathological aggravation" of a "normative crisis 'belonging' to a particular stage of individual development." This led him to ascribe a normative identity crisis to the age of adolescence and young adulthood.

Once the identity crisis was considered normative and not confined to those who had suffered a traumatic or chronic ego loss, Erikson found it necessary to define identity in broader terms. In *Identity: Youth and Crisis*, he provided two examples of "what identity feels like when you become aware of the fact that you do undoubtedly have one." The first is a statement by William James that describes the "subjective sense of an invigorating sameness and continuity" experienced by persons who have an identity. In a letter to his wife, James wrote, "A man's character is discernible in the mental or moral attitude in which, when it comes upon him, he felt himself most deeply and intensely active and alive. At such moments there is a voice inside which speaks and says: *'This* is the real me!'" In commenting on this passage, Erikson notes that James was attempting to describe the "discernment of character," but he takes the liberty of claiming that James was also describing a sense of identity—"this is the real me"—that comes upon a person as a recognition, almost as a surprise, rather than being something strenuously quested after. Identity is therefore basically a matter of self-recognition.

But this is not all that it is. Erikson's second example of "what identity feels like" is a statement by Freud that appeared in his address to the Society of B'nai B'rith in Vienna in 1926. Here Freud confessed that what bound him to Jewry was neither faith nor national pride but many obscure emotional forces and a "clear consciousness of inner identity." According to Erikson, Freud was referring to a "deep communality known only to those who shared in it, and only expressible in words more mythical than conceptual." Erikson suggests that Freud's consciousness of an "inner identity" with other Jews included a "sense of bitter pride preserved by his dispersed and other despised people throughout a long history of persecution" and a "particular (here intellectual) gift which had victoriously emerged from a hostile limitation of opportunities." Thus, Freud's sense of identity was grounded in a deep identification with his people, one that presented both a curse and a blessing: the curse of being a despised people and the blessing of a "fearless freedom of thinking."

Through the years, Erikson has given much attention to both the subjective and the communal dimensions of identity. He has made many refinements in his conception of identity as a process in the core of the individual, the major being his recent tendency to view this more as a self-reflective process and less as a matter of achieving ego synthesis.[2] He has also explored many facets of the community in the identity process, especially the adult generation's tendency to abdicate its role in the identity struggles of adolescents and young adults: "In looking at the youth of today, one is apt to forget that identity formation, while being 'critical' in youth, is really a *generational* issue. So we must not overlook what appears to be a certain abrogation of responsibility on the part of the older generation in providing those forceful ideals which must antecede identity formation in the next generation—if only so that youth can rebel against a well-defined set of older values."[3]

The negative pole of the adolescent stage crisis is identity confusion. If James and Freud capture the central meanings of identity, it is Biff in Arthur Miller's play *Death of a Salesman* who captures for Erikson the essential meaning of identity confusion: "I just can't take hold, Mom, I can't take hold of some kind of life."[4] Biff's lament captures a number of themes of identity confusion, including our inability (1) to settle on an occupational identity; (2) to hold to a commitment, often because we are aware of having made an overcommitment; (3) to perceive ourselves in one or more of the social roles valued by the adult society; and (4) to cope with the unique pressures of a society that stresses self-reliance in the earlier stages of life and yet, through its complex and centralized systems of industrial, economic, and political organization, confronts the adolescent with the prospect of institutional dependency.

Youths begin to "take hold" when they shoulder the obligation of personifying certain ideals of their community, such as Freud's commitment to the fearless freedom of thinking, which was highly valued by the community in which he was raised. To say that they shoulder the obligation, however, implies that they are responding to a moral duty and have become resigned to the fact that they are "growing up." No doubt some element of duty and resignation is involved in identity formation. But what makes it an identity process and not simply the formation of moral character (however much identity formation aids the formation of moral character) is that our adoption of these ideals is a matter of self-recognition. What is involved here is the development of a "sense of 'I.'"[5]

I have assigned the deadly sin of pride to this stage of the life cycle. Pride is often considered the chief of the deadly sins, and even as the root of all sin. The first thing to be said about pride, however, is that certain forms of pride are sinful and others are not. The first two definitions of pride in *Webster's New World Dictionary* capture the sinful nature of pride, but the third describes a desirable form of pride, and the fourth suggests a generally favorable form. Thus, pride is (1) an overhigh opinion of oneself, exaggerated self-esteem, conceit; (2) the showing of this overhigh opinion in haughty and arrogant behavior; (3) a sense of one's own dignity or worth, or self-respect; or (4) a delight or satisfaction in one's achievements, possessions, children, etc. When we say that pride is sinful, we do not mean that a sense of our own dignity and worth, or self-respect, is sinful. Nor are we saying that a simple delight or satisfaction in our achievements or possessions is sinful; the delight and satisfaction become so only when the achievements or possessions become grounds for snobbery or exclusivity. What is sinful is an exaggerated opinion of ourselves, and the showing of this in haughty or arrogant behavior. The reason that pride has both positive and negative connotations is that it refers to either a justified or an excessive belief in our worth. Only excess is sinful, though what we ourselves consider justified often seems exaggerated to others.

A number of sins branch out from pride. They include conceit, which implies an exaggerated opinion of ourselves and our achievements; vanity, which suggests an excessive desire to be admired by others for our achievements and appearance; and vainglory, a sin that is not much mentioned anymore but that implies extreme conceit manifested in boasting, swaggering, and extreme arrogance. Self-esteem, which implies a positive opinion of ourselves, is also related to pride, but there are disagreements these days as to whether self-esteem is a sin or an appropriate expression of personal dignity and worth.[6] For Erikson, self-esteem is not only appropriate but also essential to the formation of identity. For the adolescent whose identity is beginning to take form, self-esteem becomes a "conviction that one is learning effective steps toward a tangible future, that one is developing a defined personality within a social reality which one understands."[7] Thus self-esteem is not an exalted opinion of ourselves but an "accrued confidence" in our "individual way of mastering experience." This corresponds with Henry Fairlie's view that "a reasonable and justified self-esteem is not what is meant by the sin of Pride."[8] As Stanford Lyman puts it, "Poised somewhere between sinful vanity and self-destructive submissiveness is a golden mean of self-esteem appropriate to the human condition."[9]

Chaucer's parson says that the deadly sin of pride takes many forms, including arrogance, impudence, boasting, hypocrisy, and joy in having done harm. According to the parson, pride may be inward or outward. But he is mainly concerned with its outward forms, such as wearing too many clothes or too few, carrying one's body in a seductive manner, employing many servants, and offering ostentatious hospitality. The parson does not discuss inward forms of pride, nor does he describe pride as a basic attitude or disposition toward life.

But Fairlie does. In his analysis of pride, Fairlie focuses on the basic attitude of pride. In the course of his discussion, he relates pride to all three dispositional roots of sin, including rebellion, isolation, and personal bondage. He says that we associate pride, more than any other sin, with *rebellion*. Pride calls to mind the rebellion of "our first parents," Adam and Eve. Our primordial parents were exalted in themselves; otherwise they would not have succumbed to the temptation set before them. Self-elevated, they also became rash and self-willed. Thus pride is the original cause of disobedience, of the flouting of legitimate authority. The proud person feels no obligation to respect the authority of another, because the proud are authorities unto themselves.

Pride is also a form of *isolation*, because it is a form of self-love in which we deny our need for the community of others: "The proud man sets himself apart. A tower is one of the commonest metaphors of Pride. It is lofty and inaccessible." The prideful, then, are best described as aloof and unreachable by others. They do not consider themselves part of common humanity but instead turn away from society. Pride "is a sin of neglect: It provokes us to ignore others. It is the sin of aggression: It provokes us to hurt others. It is a sin of condescension: It makes us patronize others." The prideful refuse to acknowledge the obligations of human society and deny a need for community with others. When involvement with others does occur, it is based on competition: "Pride must be competitive, since it cannot bear to concede first place to anyone else, even when its real wants are satisfied."[10]

Pride is also a form of *personal bondage,* because it is self-alienating. Pride cuts us off not only from human society but also from what in our own natures we should most deeply know and enjoy. This is a particularly serious problem in our time, because we are taught to exalt our own personality and yet we search that personality only very shallowly: "We have only to look at ourselves to see what tedious and trivial chroniclers we have become of our selves and our lives. We exalt what is little more than a self-intriguing but idle curiosity about ourselves into the pretense that we are seriously engaged in trying to know ourselves."[11] Thus, prideful persons distance themselves from dimensions of themselves that may challenge their high opinion of themselves or require them to acknowledge emotional needs that can be met only by other persons. Their personal bondage and their isolation go hand in hand.

This personal bondage is especially evident in adolescents. Fairlie acknowledges that "this self-centeredness of the young is engaging in a way. It is natural that they should be interested in finding out who and what they are."[12] But adult society has encouraged the self-centeredness of youth and has even imitated their condition. Adults' programs for "self-improvement" often foster self-centeredness by measuring the improvement according to how good we feel about ourselves, and not in terms of our contribution to the well-being of others. Thus pride is rooted in a basic narcissism in which individuals, like Narcissus in the Greek myth, are essentially in love with themselves and incapable of loving others. Similarly, for Lyman the narcissist is "the true isolate," who "takes no object for his own love except himself."[13] Here again personal bondage and isolation are two sides of the same coin, and both are the consequences of pride.

How then does pride relate to the crisis of identity versus identity confusion? Fairlie's comments on the pridefulness of youth provide welcome support for my decision to link pride to the adolescent stage of the life cycle. The primary basis for the linkage is the fact that pride in its sinful form is an excessive self-centeredness. A certain self-centeredness is appropriate to youth in this stage. As Fairlie notes, "It is natural that they should be interested in finding out who and what they are." This, of course, is what discovering one's identity is: it is a matter of self-recognition. But identity has two major aspects—its subjective and its social sides. One's identity is not formed or discerned in isolation from other persons and groups. Thus, identity is an affirmation of a certain kind of self-centeredness (a *subjective* view of oneself) without the excesses of pride (a *privatistic* view of oneself). In this sense, the discernment of one's own identity is diametrically opposed to pride.

Pride fosters personal bondage, an alienation from aspects of ourselves. In contrast, the discovery of our identity involves breaking out of this bondage and recognizing dimensions of ourselves that we were previously ashamed to recognize or acknowledge. Pride fosters isolation from human society. In contrast, the discovery of one's identity involves making at least tentative commitments to certain values and social roles provided by the community. The adolescent who is unable to entertain such commitments will often take refuge in an attitude and perhaps even overt acts of rebellion. As self-centeredness is natural for adolescents, some degree of rebellion is too. But there is a difference between rebellion that grows out of an effort to discern what values are worth committing oneself to (the self-recognition of identity), and rebellion that repudiates values for the sake of repudia-

tion alone (pride). Thus, here too the discovery of one's identity involves dissociating oneself from the rebellion of pride.

In the final analysis, the solution to the identity crisis of adolescence
is religious. Each individual needs to "feel that I am the center of
awareness in a universe of experience in which I have a coherent
identity."[14] But, for Erikson, this "sense of 'I'" can ultimately be confirmed only by God, who is the eternal center of awareness. Thus, as
religions have always taught, the answer to the exaggerated self-centeredness of pride is to become centered in God. This recentering is
based on the conviction that God, not I, is the eternal Self, the Center
of the Universe. But it does not follow that engaging in self-reflection
is no longer appropriate. On the contrary, the awareness of the eternal
Self enables us to reflect more deeply on who we are, on what it
means for our lives that we are created in the image and likeness of
God.

Young Adulthood and the Deadly Sin of Lust

The adult stages have a longer duration than the childhood and adolescent stages and therefore involve considerable psychodynamic
complexity. For this reason, it is probably best to view the psychosocial themes of intimacy versus isolation, generativity versus stagnation, and integrity versus despair as dynamically decisive for these
stages but not exhaustive of the conflicts and crises normally experienced in them.

In young adulthood, we are confronted with the developmental crisis of intimacy versus isolation. The capacity for true intimacy is probably only possible when identity formation is well on its way. Adolescents and young adults who are unsure of their identities shy away
from interpersonal intimacy, or they throw themselves into acts of intimacy that are promiscuous, without true commitment and genuine
self-abandon. But young adults whose identities are taking shape are
ready for genuine intimacy. Emerging from the discernment of identity, however fragile and tentative that may be, young adults are eager
and willing to fuse their newly discovered identities with the identities of others. They are ready for intimacy—ready to commit themselves to concrete affiliations and partnerships and to develop the ethical strength to abide by such commitments even though that may call
for significant sacrifices and compromises.[15]

Intimacy in young adulthood may take a number of forms. The primary form involves a "loved partner" with whom we are able and

willing to share a mutual trust and to regulate our cycles of work, procreation, and recreation. Other forms of intimacy include close friendships, close relationships with mentors, and closeness with the "recesses of the self." In each of these forms of intimacy, we take chances with the identity we formed in the preceding stage. Isolation, the negative pole of this stage, means the inability to take chances with our identities by sharing true intimacy. Isolation often takes the form of withdrawal from others, but it is also reflected in competitive and combative behavior toward those with whom we also share intimacies.

Thus intimacy and isolation are often deeply entangled in young adulthood. Intimate and combative relations are experienced with and against the same persons. Many young adults have difficulty separating the combative encounter and the erotic bond. This is especially common in new marriages, in which there are often both affirmation and repudiation, desire and abuse. The impulse toward isolation is also reflected in the tendency of some young married couples to withdraw into their own world (dyadic withdrawal) and to pay little attention to the world around them. That is a form of intimacy, but it occurs in the context of severe isolation. As Erikson puts it, "There are partnerships which amount to an isolation à deux, protecting both partners from the necessity to face the next critical development— that of generativity."[16]

I have linked the deadly sin of lust to the young adult stage, and thus to the conflict of intimacy versus isolation. By definition, lust is (1) a desire to gratify the senses; (2) a sexual desire, often implying the desire for unrestrained gratification; or (3) an overmastering desire, as a lust for power. Most writers on the deadly sin of lust center on sexual desires. They give little attention to the lust for power, or to the relationships between sexual lust and the lust for power.

Chaucer's parson says that lust is a "near cousin" to gluttony. Fairlie supports this association of lust and gluttony, pointing out that lust is interested not in its partners but "only in the appeasement of an appetite that we are unable to subdue."[17] What is more, sexual lust, like gluttony, is a form of self-subjection, because it involves no real choices (i.e., choice of a partner) but accepts what is available. In addition, it is a form of self-abdication, because it surrenders our need and ability to give and receive. Lust seeks a momentary gratification. Love, the counterpart to lust, has sufficient continuance, allowing us to know someone else with intimacy and sharing. But lust envisions no continuity of relationship; it lives for the moment of gratification and then returns to its solitude. Unlike love, which intends involvement, lust will not get involved, refusing to accept responsibility for the consequences of the sexual act.[18]

Kenneth Slack indicts lust for many of the same reasons that Fairlie does. But he adds that lust usually involves cruelty, both physical and mental. Rape is the most extreme example of lust's cruelty, but cruelty usually accompanies even the seemingly more benign forms of lust. We must therefore be careful in our sexually permissive society not to condone lust or minimize its seriousness, because in the real world lust and cruelty coexist: "Sometimes the cruelty takes the form of exploitation, sometimes it is the great cruelty of betrayal of deep levels of trust, sometimes strong affections and passions are evoked only to be finally rejected and broken off. Again and again, in Harry Williams' words, lust is 'an attempt to snatch value for myself from somebody else': all such greedy snatching can be an act of plain cruelty."[19]

In his discussion of lust, Lyman analyzes the views of major Christian theologians, including Augustine, Aquinas, Luther, and the Puritan tradition. His analysis indicates that theologians see the need to control lust but reach little consensus on how this should be accomplished. Some, like Luther and the Puritans, believe that individuals can learn control through God's assistance. Others advocate institutional constraints, either because the individual is incapable of personal restraint (Augustine) or because the individual needs assistance in the struggle (Aquinas). Lyman extends his analysis to contemporary social theorists who as moralists worry about lust and its effects on society. They do not discuss lust directly, but by emphasizing the importance of love to the formation and maintenance of healthy societies, they do so indirectly. Underlying contemporary discussions of the positive effects of monogamous marriage, nuclear family structures, and heterosexual relationships, there is a deep but unacknowledged uneasiness about the social consequences of lust. Lust is dysfunctional, because it "can consume the totality of interests, activities, and energies of those overwhelmed by it."[20] Lust, with its potential for monopolizing our energies and interests, may drive out all other social linkages. For this reason, societies with diverse cultures have sought to weaken the opportunities and inhibit the passions that lead to the departure from duty.[21] Thus, for contemporary social theorists, as for Christian theologians, lust is not just a personal matter but a sin against society. The major difficulty with lust from the social point of view is that it inhibits our capacity to perform our social roles and to carry out our social responsibilities.

Lust then is a sin against ourselves (self-subjection, self-abdication), against other persons (cruelty, exploitation), and against society (irresponsibility). In all three aspects, lust is solitary and disloyal.

I have assigned lust to the young-adult stage of life cycle and thus rooted it dynamically in the conflict of intimacy versus isolation. My point is not that young adults necessarily exhibit greater lustful behavior than other adults, or even adolescents. Rather, my point is that lust, as an attitude toward life, is rooted in the dynamics of the conflict of intimacy versus isolation. Lust is an enemy of intimacy and is also a very destructive form of isolation. Intimacy is the capacity to commit ourselves to other persons and to abide by such commitments. In contrast, lust envisions no continuity of relationship. It lives only for the moment of gratification. Intimacy reflects a willingness to fuse our identity with another's in an act of genuine self-abandon. In contrast, lust is a form of self-subjection (no real choice of a partner) and self-abdication (no real giving of oneself or receiving of another self). Intimacy is also essential to the carrying out of social responsibilities, especially in relation to adult generativity (i.e., the procreation and care of children). In contrast, lust, because it is profoundly isolationist, inhibits our capacity to carry out the role of generative adults.

Unfortunately, lust is not always easy to identify, because intimate and combative relations are often experienced with and against the same persons. This enables lust to masquerade as intimacy. Lust can rather easily be discerned for what it is in the case of gang rape; it is less easy to identify in relations between two "loving partners." But there are identifiable signs of lust even in relationships where intimacy is present: especially disloyalty, cruelty, and an unwillingness to assume responsibility for the consequences of one's actions. Thus lust is allied with isolation but often assumes the guise of intimacy. The church has tried to combat this deceitfulness by identifying lust's characteristics and unmasking its motivations. The church has also supported other social institutions that appear to contain or control lust, especially the social institutions of marriage and the family. But these institutions have not been able to protect individuals or the society from the destructive effects of lust. In many cases, they have merely domesticated it. Luther's view that marriage may be the remedy for lust has proved overly optimistic, since lust is found in the marriage relationship itself, often in the form of overt physical violence.

But though these efforts to combat lust have not been very successful, the church has been correct in its view that lust rivals pride as the deadliest of sins. If pride reflects inordinate self-regard, lust reflects total disregard for others. And common to both is a deep sense of self-alienation. By constructing a grandiose image of ourselves, pride inhibits our ability to experience, recognize, and value the "real me." In a similar way, lust surrenders the opportunity to know ourselves through the giving of ourselves to another.

The Dispositional Roots of Pride and Lust

The two deadly sins discussed in this chapter reflect all three roots of sin—rebellion, personal bondage, and isolation. Pride rebels against legitimate authority. Lust reflects a rebellious impulse-life where passions are out of control. Pride reflects the personal bondage of narcissism. Lust reflects the personal bondage of self-subjection and self-abdication. Pride isolates us from human society through a sense of superiority and arrogance. Lust isolates us from human society through its cruel and exploitative approach to individuals and its irresponsible attitude toward social obligations. Thus, pride and lust reflect all three roots of sin.

But the central root of pride is personal bondage—imprisonment by a rather spurious form of self-love. And the basic root of lust is isolation. We miss much of what makes these two sins deadly when we view pride mainly in terms of rebellion and lust in terms of personal bondage. It is true that prideful persons rebel against external authority. But this is largely a consequence of their personal bondage, their inability to break out of themselves and accept their dependency on others. And it may be true that lustful persons are in bondage to their passions and therefore unable to control themselves. But such bondage is ultimately due to deep antisocial attitudes, to a refusal to relate to another in terms of mutual giving and receiving and to accept responsibility for the consequences of one's actions.

Together, pride and lust point to the deadliness of the deadly sins by demonstrating the inadequacy of social controls for restraining the sins. Pride places itself above such controls, and lust places itself outside them. Recognizing that social controls cannot adequately contain the two sins, the Puritan tradition made much use of personal self-examination to combat them. The same weapon is available to us today. But today much so-called self-examination is designed to make people feel good about themselves. It is shallow and undiscerning. This is also true of much counseling. As James Gustafson points out, "My impression, which might be distorted, is that a great deal of counseling, pastoral and otherwise, is oriented toward the relieving of anxiety, stress, and overburdening senses of guilt. In contrast with this, serious attention to moral matters can often increase anxiety, stress, and the sense of guilt."[22] Clearly, we need more effective resources against the deadly sins.

In this book, I draw particular attention to the resources available to us from our religious heritage. Especially powerful among the resources for cultivating the virtuous life are the teachings of Jesus (the Beatitudes) and the narrative tradition of the Bible (which enables us to view the church not as an instrument of social control but as a way of life). We should not discount the value of self-examination for combating the deadly sins in our lives. But self-examination can be shallow and subject to all sorts of distortions when it occurs in a moral and spiritual vacuum. Its effectiveness depends on its being supported by resources derived from the community of faith. Otherwise it reflects the same privatistic and isolationist spirit that we find in the deadly sins themselves.

CHAPTER FIVE

The Sins of Middle and Mature Adulthood

The two remaining stages of the life cycle are middle adulthood, with its crisis of generativity versus stagnation, and mature adulthood, with its crisis of integrity versus despair. I have assigned the sin of apathy to middle adulthood and the sin of melancholy to mature adulthood. As I noted in chapter 1, these two sins were originally considered distinct but were later fused into one. I believe that they are sufficiently different from each other that they deserve independent status. Nonetheless, by placing them in contiguous stages of the life cycle, I honor the traditional view that they are in fact closely related to each other.

Middle Adulthood and the
Deadly Sin of Apathy

The developmental crisis of middle adulthood involves generativity versus stagnation. By generativity, Erikson means a concern for establishing and guiding the next generation. This may involve parental responsibilities, but the term "generativity" means much more than the parental role. Some persons, through misfortune or conscious choice, do not have offspring of their own. Yet they can be as generative as, or even more generative than, those who have responsibility for their own children. For Erikson, generativity is a matter of caring for whatever is being generated, attending to its nurture and growth.[1]

Generativity is also more than productivity and creativity. Generativity includes these, but it involves a continuing emotional investment in what is being generated. Whereas productivity focuses on the

58

making of things, and creativity focuses on the generative act itself, generativity centers on the care and nurture of what has already been produced or created. Generativity is a driving power in all human organization, for *"all* institutions by their very nature codify the ethics of generative succession."[2] But schools are the primary social institutions in which adults are directly involved in the generative process, training the younger generation in the proven methods and accrued wisdom of the society so that they can take their place in the succession of generations. Monastic communities also have a special relationship to generativity, because they renounce the right to procreate in order to center attention on "ultimate concerns." Central to the monastic life is the discernment of the Care that grounds all existence.[3]

The negative pole of this stage is stagnation, which occurs when individuals are unable to invest themselves emotionally in what is being generated. Stagnation is the inability to sustain interest in the products or fruits of our generativity, whether this involves children or the work of our hands and minds. The sense of stagnation, usually accompanied by boredom and interpersonal impoverishment, often takes the form of self-indulgence. This is a kind of pseudoparenting, for such individuals "often begin to indulge themselves as if they were their own . . . one and only child."[4] Stagnation also takes the form of self-absorption, a preoccupation with our own needs that makes it difficult to respond to the needs of others. Such self-absorption can produce a premature invalidism, either physical or psychological, which leads to increased self-concern and increased inability to care for others.

Thus stagnation has a variety of consequences, both for the individual who is supposed to be generative and for the persons who are meant to be helped or nurtured by that individual. The effects of stagnation are dynamically similar to "burnout," since burnout is usually defined as the loss of interest, respect, or sympathy for those for whom we are responsible.

The deadly sin of apathy is rooted in the dynamics of generativity versus stagnation. By linking apathy to this conflict, we are able to recover the central meaning of apathy, rescuing it from the word "sloth," which is commonly used to name this sin. The word "sloth" implies an unwillingness to work or exert ourselves, a sluggishness, indolence, or laziness. That does not adequately capture the meaning of the word "apathy." "Apathy" has a variety of meanings, including negligence, indifference, restlessness, listlessness and boredom, misery and dejection. Sloth or laziness may be one behavioral manifestation of certain aspects of apathy, but sloth does not get to the root of the issue, nor does it convey just how serious the problem of apathy can be: "By sloth in our everyday idiom we mean only idleness, and idleness can be attractive, even something that is worth cultivating."[5] In a world of busy activity and hyperactivity, sloth may well be a positive virtue. At the least, it seems a fairly harmless vice. But apathy is never positive, and rarely harmless. To be apathetic is to be dispirited, empty of feeling. In its more extreme forms, it is a living death. When we call this deadly sin sloth, the multiplicity of meanings associated with apathy is also lost. But that multiplicity is itself important, since one reason apathy is so difficult to identify as such is that it takes so many different forms.

The word in the English language that comes closest to the central meaning of the word *acedia*, which is what this sin was originally called, is "apathy." But indifference is also a very important aspect of *acedia*. Both apathy and indifference mean a lack of interest. But indifference adds a lack of concern or feeling, especially with regard to a distressing situation, and apathy adds a lack of emotion and a listless condition. Thus both apathy and indifference involve an inability to take interest in what we would normally be expected to have an interest or investment in. But indifference is mainly concerned with what this means for those who are the victims of our lack of interest, whereas apathy focuses on the psychological (and spiritual) condition of the person who is unable or unwilling to take an interest. Together then the words "apathy" and "indifference" capture the major meanings of *acedia*. Although the best English word for *acedia* is "apathy," the fact that "apathy" does not capture all the meanings of *acedia* leads most writers on the deadly sins to use the Latin word itself.

As Stanford Lyman points out, *acedia* first emerges as an alienation of the self from the world and then develops into a self-alienation. The most extreme form of *acedia* is a withdrawal from all participation in the care of others and even the care of ourselves. Less extreme forms include idleness, tardiness, negligence, indolence, and irritability. In medieval literature, *acedia* is associated with motionlessness, and is depicted as the feet of the devil that halt persons in their tracks. It is also portrayed as a languishing and holding back, a refusal to undertake good works because the personal costs seem too high or the prospects of success seem too low. And it was said to slow down the mind, inhibiting its attention to matters of real importance.

Acedia takes both passive and active forms. Its passive forms are the more visible, but their evil nature is not quite so easy to discern. They are reflected in lethargy, lifelessness, and paralysis of the will. The passive form of *acedia* is the experience of Christian monks, many of whom view *acedia* as the most dangerous and insidious of the deadly sins. The high incidence of passive *acedia* among monks may be attributable to the fact that their lives are centered on the hope of the life hereafter and thus the present life is of relatively little value. Too, the monastic life is centered on meditation and contemplation, and the active life is rejected or renounced. As a result, there is the potential for lethargy and listlessness, not only in the performance of necessary and unavoidable earthly tasks but also and especially in the life of prayer itself. Monks lament the fact that they can no longer take interest in God and that, once this happens, they are caught in a vicious circle, for as their interest in God begins to wane, they lack the means to revive it.[6] *Acedia* is the sin that "believes in nothing, cares for nothing, seeks to know nothing, interferes with nothing, enjoys nothing, hates nothing, finds purpose in nothing, lives for nothing, and remains alive because there is nothing for which it will die."[7]

Christians who have reflected seriously on the sin of *acedia* have recognized that the ultimate answer to the vicious circle is some form of spiritual regeneration in which we are again moved by the indwelling spirit of God. If we view *acedia* only in terms of sloth or laziness, we imply that this is a sin under our own control. But the very impassivity that *acedia* effects leaves us impotent to combat the sin. Thus, in its passive form *acedia* reveals a spiritual emptiness and our need for spiritual regeneration.

The more active forms of *acedia* involve a sense of boredom and a restlessness of the spirit. In discussing the active forms, Lyman focuses on the Olympian gods. Because they were highly anthropomorphic, the Olympian deities are good examples of how *acedia* appears in human society. Their boredom and restlessness are due to the fact that they have no need of hope, for all their desires have already been met. So instead of applying themselves to the realization of their desires, they become bored and restless. As a result, they begin to meddle in human affairs, not because they are genuinely interested in what humans are about but as a way of achieving some personal amusement and distraction from their boredom. They also begin to devise clever plots for obstructing the gratification of the desires of other gods, and this creates an atmosphere of gratuitous conflict, conspiracies, intrigue, and deceit. Thus the effect of *acedia* in its more active forms of boredom and restlessness is to make life needlessly troublesome and difficult for other people. The television drama "Dallas" is a good example of the needless havoc people create for one another when they are bored and restless. It also explains why sloth and laziness are associated with *acedia*, since the problem with the main characters in

"Dallas" is that they do not have enough to do. If they had useful work, they would not have time to meddle in other people's business.

Thus, for *acedia* in its more active forms hard work is a particularly valuable antidote. At least, hard work reduces the socially destructive effects of *acedia*. Nevertheless, this solution does not get to the root of the problem, to the personal desires that promote boredom and restlessness. If *acedia* in its passive form is the absence of desire, *acedia* in its active form involves a distortion of desires. Such distortion is usually attributable to problems in the timing of the gratification of desires. Instant or premature gratification leads to boredom, because there is nothing more to hope and work for. But long delayed or elusive gratification leads to hopelessness, and permanently delayed or denied gratification leads to despair.

The distinction between passive and active forms of *acedia* is useful for many purposes, but it is particularly valuable for clarifying the differences between apathy and indifference. The attitude that underlies passive *acedia* is apathy, a lack of emotion and a listless condition. Here, we are unmoved and immobilized. The attitude that underlies active *acedia* is indifference, our disregard for a distressing situation and our unconcern that we are contributors to the distress of others. What unites these two forms of *acedia* is their common lack of interest, as expressed in the attitude, Who cares?

I suggest that the sin of *acedia*, with its two aspects of apathy and indifference, is rooted dynamically in the conflict of generativity versus stagnation. Generativity is the concern for establishing and guiding the next generation and is the concern that should undergird and therefore take precedence over all other adult interests and projects. The sin of *acedia* reflects a profound lack of interest in those who have been entrusted to our care. In its apathetic form, it means a debilitating preoccupation with our own self and a spiritual withdrawal from the next generation and its concerns and problems. In its form of indifference, it means inhibiting the younger generation's growth in an arbitrary, capricious, and even malicious way. Because it is so all-encompassing, the sin of *acedia* involves more than a lack of concern for the next generation. It reflects a lack of concern for life itself. But virtually all the socially constructive activity of middle adults directly or indirectly involves caring and making provision for the rising generation. When we lose interest in the concerns and aspirations of the next generation, this is a clear sign that *acedia* has begun to take control over us. Its effects may not be immediately apparent, because an adult may find any number of ways to remain interested in life apart from an interest in establishing the next generation. But in time it will become apparent how shallow these interests actually are, because they are not rooted in any social or cosmic network of care.

Thus, *acedia* and stagnation are virtually synonymous. Stagnant adults are apathetic. They are self-absorbed, imprisoned in their own narrow self-indulgence, and suffering from boredom and interpersonal impoverishment. They are also potential psychological and even physical invalids. This is consistent with traditional descriptions of *acedia* as a kind of motionlessness, an inability to move about or to be moved within by the indwelling spirit of God. So the deadly sin of *acedia* grows out of a failure in generativity. The truly generative adult has a sustained emotional investment in what is being generated. The acedic adult has no such investment, is unable to care. The initial losers are those who rely on the goodwill of adults responsible for their care and support. The eventual losers are the acedic adults themselves as they become interpersonally impoverished and spiritually empty.

There is no simple remedy for *acedia*. In *Young Man Luther*, Erikson suggests that Luther's great "theological breakthrough" occurred when he discovered that he could not cure himself through self-initiated programs of personal renewal but that he needed to wait upon the Lord and allow the spirit of God to move within him and move him to action.[8] Erikson suggests that we have a physiological analogue for this spiritual process in the movement of bowels, which are traditionally associated with compassion (Erikson notes that Luther was a lifelong sufferer from constipation), but even more illustratively, in the activity of the fetus in a woman's uterus.[9] In both cases, but especially in the latter, the movement within is a matter not of our own will or intention but of a process beyond our conscious control. *Acedia* is a spiritual crisis, and the only solution to the crisis is a spiritual renewal through which the spirit of God moves within us and moves us to care again. On the other hand, though we cannot force the spirit to move within us and restore us to life again, we can open ourselves to the spirit and be receptive to it. As Erikson points out in *Young Man Luther*, the Bible was for Luther the avenue through which he opened himself to the spirit of God. The Bible became, as it were, a second mother to Luther, enabling him to experience a spiritual rebirth.

Mature Adulthood and the Deadly Sin of Melancholy

The psychosocial conflict of mature adulthood centers upon integrity versus despair. Erikson has expressed a reluctance to try to define what integrity means, but he has pointed to a few of its attributes. First of all, integrity reflects an assurance, developed through a long life-time, of our proclivity for order and meaning. In his earliest presentation of his life-cycle theory, Erikson described this proclivity, somewhat vaguely, as an assurance of "some world order and spiritual sense."[10] In later versions, he has called it an "emotional integration" that tries to be "faithful to the image-bearers of the past" and "is ready to take, and eventually to renounce, leadership in the present."[11] Common to both renderings is the perception that we are participants in a larger world order and the assurance that such a perception is inherently true. The world order involves the whole history of human culture. In addition, it has a transcendent dimension to which the image bearers of the past have testified.

A second attribute of integrity is an acceptance of our own life cycle and an acceptance of the people who have become significant to it. This aspect of integrity focuses on our love for others, especially for our parents, whom we release from the wish that they had been different and from the claim that they are responsible for what we have become. Instead we accept personal responsibility for our life even as we recognize that it has been "something that had to be" and that "permitted of no substitutions." Morally we become our own fathers and mothers, responsible for the self that we have begotten, raised, and brought to fruition.[12]

A third attribute of integrity is a "sense of comradeship with men and women of distant times and of different pursuits who have created orders and objects and sayings conveying human dignity and love."[13] If the second attribute of integrity centers on our membership in a specific human family with its particular destiny, the third attribute centers on our sense of comradeship with the generative women and men of other times, other places, and other pursuits. Numbered among these men and women are the special image bearers to whom we have attempted to be faithful. But the third attribute of integrity points to the larger community of men and women whose identities may not be known to us but whose lives were truly generative. As we anticipate our own anonymity after we pass from this earth, there is comfort in knowing that we are the comrades of many anonymous but generative people who have gone before us and who also tried to live lives of human dignity and love.

A fourth attribute of integrity is a personal sense of coherence or wholeness, linking the three organizing processes of *soma* (or body), *psyche* (or mind), and *ethos* (or intergenerational experience).[14] Owing to the tendency of these three processes to disintegrate in old age, we need to be able to discern how all the previous life stages hold together, and how the last stage permits the integrative experience of earlier stages to come to fruition. The sense of the thread of continuity in our life throughout the stages is a major resource in "keeping things together" in the last stage of life.

The attributes of integrity make clear that integrity is not a rare quality of personal character but a "shared proclivity for understanding or for 'hearing' those who do understand, the integrative ways of human life."[15] Integrity is not a special trait or achievement but a sensitivity to the various elements that give order and continuity to human life. Integrity is a way of seeing, of perceiving the order in our lives, in human experience generally, and in the cosmos itself—an order that is there to be seen if we have eyes to see it.

What is despair, the negative pole of the eighth stage of the life cycle? It is the inability to accept our particular life cycle as something that had to be and that permitted no substitutions. To despair is to look back on the course of our life with regret, lamenting that it took the form it did, and perhaps even regretting that we were ever born. Despair "expresses the feeling that the time is short, too short for the attempt to start another life and to try out alternate roads to integrity." Such despair is "often hidden behind a show of disgust, a misanthropy, or a chronic contemptuous displeasure with particular institutions and particular people—a disgust and a displeasure which . . . signify the individual's contempt of himself."[16] This does not mean that all expressions of disgust and displeasure by older persons are rooted in despair, for some experiences in life, especially in mature adulthood, warrant displeasure and disgust. Despair is present, however, when disgust and displeasure are not balanced by constructive ideas, cooperation with others, and faith in the future.

In his most recent comments on the eighth stage of life, Erikson admits that despair may seem more immediately convincing than integrity. After all, the last stage of life "marks the total end . . . of this, our one given course of life," and it is finally unpredictable when and how the end will happen. The fact that our life will soon end, and in an unpredictable way, gives ample grounds for despair. Furthermore, the discontinuity of family life as a result of dislocation contributes to the lack in old age of what is necessary for staying "really alive." All this is further exacerbated when we carry over a continuing sense of stagnation from the previous stage. There is also the personal mourning that occurs in the final stage of life, mourning "not only for time forfeited and space depleted but also . . . for autonomy weakened, initiative lost, intimacy missed, generativity neglected" and "identity potentials by-passed or, indeed, an all too limiting identity lived."[17] Given these manifold invitations to despair, it is understandable that older persons often defend against despair by "mythologizing" their own lives in a way that in some cases amounts to a "pseudointegration."[18] The better defense against despair, however, is not to mythologize our lives but to envision them in relation to the ongoing succession of genera-tions—in those who have gone before us and those who will come af-ter us.

The deadly sin of melancholy is related, dynamically, to this eighth stage of the life cycle. Since contemporary discussions of the deadly sins include only seven sins, melancholy has not received much atten-tion. But both Lyman and Henry Fairlie include a brief discussion of melancholy in their analyses of the sin of sloth. Fairlie discusses melan-choly in relation to what he calls the "condition of desirelessness that is Sloth." He asks, What is the source of this condition of desireless-ness? What is responsible for our tendency to "reduce our desires to the shallowest of levels, so that we can then persuade ourselves that we have satisfied them?"[19] He contends that such desirelessness is ul-timately rooted in despair of God's creation. We lack passion for life, for enhancing its goodness and beauty, because we view the world of God's creation with despair and even disgust. But our despair is not based on a true perception of the world. It is just as distorted as the view that the world is a thoroughly wonderful place.

Fairlie then develops an analysis of Kierkegaard's melancholy, not-ing that melancholy was largely responsible for Kierkegaard's ten-dency toward a despairing view of the world and for the desireless-ness that results from this despair. But he also contends that because Kierkegaard was aware of his tendency to despair, he worked doubly hard to combat it through a lifelong refusal to renounce the life of pas-sionate desire. Thus Fairlie roots the deadly sin of melancholy in a de-spairing attitude toward life in which we relinquish all but the most in-consequential desires.

Lyman also develops a brief analysis of melancholy in his discussion of sloth, noting that Gregory the Great included "rancor," a continuing and bitter hate or ill will, among the consequences of melancholy. By exploring the relationship between rancor and melancholy, Lyman demonstrates the destructive side of melancholy, thus distinguishing it from simple sadness. His exploration takes him to the psychoana-lytic tradition and to the "discovery of cloaked anger and unconscious hostility at the base of the melancholic attitude."[20]

According to Freudian theory, both mourning and melancholy have their origins in the loss of a loved object. In the mourning process, we withdraw interest and investment from that object. This is a normal reaction to the loss. But mourning may go further, toward an abnormal melancholic attitude. That happens when we become enraged with the loved one for leaving us. The rage may in turn give rise to sadistic thoughts and feelings toward the loved object, desiring its hurt and even fantasizing ourselves as inflicting pain on the other.

The Freudian view of melancholy as avenging the loss of a loved object supports Gregory the Great's association of melancholy and rancor. In this view, mourning and melancholy are very different responses to loss. Mourners accept the loss of the loved object but continue to remember its presence and long for its return. Melancholics cannot accept the loss but instead want to avenge it and are filled with resentment and hate. Because the opportunities to avenge the loss are few and unsatisfactory, melancholics tend to internalize their rage, directing it at themselves or directing it toward other human objects, especially persons associated in some way with the lost object.

As Fairlie focuses on Kierkegaard, Lyman centers on Hamlet, another melancholic Dane, to illustrate the tragic consequences of melancholy: "While others go through a normal period of mourning for the dead king, Hamlet sinks into melancholy." And his melancholy feeds and is fed by despair: "Melancholia not infrequently leads to violence and aggression. . . . For Hamlet, however, it leads to withdrawal, self-doubt, and uncertainty. Hamlet has lost faith in his world, and in himself." He condemns the world, viewing it with disgust and disdain.[21]

These analyses of melancholy support the idea that this sin belongs to the stage of the life cycle typified by the conflict of integrity versus despair. The eighth stage of life involves considerable loss, much of it directly related to the gains of earlier stages of the life cycle. Some of these losses have to do with regret for not making more of life's opportunities than we might have ("identity potentials bypassed" and "generativity neglected"). Other losses relate to the inevitable diminishments of old age, including the loss or diminishment of autonomy, initiative, and intimacy. It is normal for us to mourn the curtailment of our autonomy and the necessity of new dependencies, the drying up of opportunities for initiative, especially in the continuing pursuit of our occupation or profession, and the loss or absence of intimacy due to the death of our spouse or to physical or mental disability. These are real and generally permanent losses, and they cause pain, sometimes more than we can bear. If the pain of the losses leads some older persons to melancholy, it is hardly appropriate for others to castigate them moralistically. Of all the deadly sins, melancholy exacts its own punishment.

But it is appropriate for us to note the critical differences between mourning and melancholy and to recognize the self-destructive effects of melancholy. Persons who are melancholic turn against what has been lost and treat it with disdain and disgust. They defend against their loss by declaring (falsely, of course) that they did not really love it anyway. This amounts to a condemnation of what has been lost, and a self-condemnation for previous investments in it. The consequence of such melancholy is that we cannot look back on our life with assurance of its order, meaning, and coherence—of its essential integrity. Instead, the whole course of our life is now viewed with despair. Our "one and only life cycle" is not accepted but repudiated. Often the persons who played significant roles in shaping our lives, and the generative individuals of distant times and different pursuits with whom we might otherwise have identified ourselves, are also repudiated.

Thus the deadly sin of melancholy is at the very center of the crisis of integrity versus despair, prompting those who have suffered grievous losses to turn against the world and against their own participation in it. To succumb to melancholy is to relinquish any vision we might have had of the integrity of our lives, because melancholy demands that we reject any claims to the value or meaning of our earlier investments.

Usually a melancholic attitude does not suddenly emerge in the last stage of life. The disposition toward melancholy has roots in the apathy and indifference of the previous stage. Even as the grounds for despair in the eighth stage are laid in the stagnation of the seventh stage, and the integrity of the eighth stage is prefigured in the generativity of the seventh, there are very strong dynamic links between the apathy and indifference of the seventh stage and the melancholy of the eighth. Where melancholy rules, apathy and indifference are intensified. Apathy as a lack of feeling for ourselves becomes self-contempt, and indifference as disregard for others becomes hatred and ill will.

Common sense might tell us that a lack of interest or investment in life during the middle adult years will make it easier to bear the losses of our later years: less investment, less pain. But the truth is precisely the opposite. What makes our losses bearable—the object of mourning, not melancholy—is that they are part of a total process of integrity formation in which we are learning new ways and objects of love. These include a new and different kind of love for the significant others in our lives, for generative men and women of distant times and places, and not least of all, for the person we have ourselves turned out to be. Loved objects are lost and longed for, but love endures and indeed assumes new and different forms. So integrity, the major gain experienced in a period involving much loss, has its basis in the generativity of our middle years, when we learned genuinely to care for others. In mature adulthood, the caring of the previous stage is the basis for our expanded and even deeper capacity to love in spite of our losses.

The Dispositional Roots of
Acedia and Melancholy

The sin of *acedia* is grounded in all three roots of sin—rebellion, personal bondage, and isolation. When we are apathetic, we are usually in some state of *isolation*, emotionally removed or distant from what is going on around us. And when we are indifferent, we often express this indifference in some form of *rebellion* (overt or covert) against the legitimate claims that others place upon us. But the root of sin that best captures the dispositional core of *acedia* is *self-bondage*, the inability to break out of our inner prison and to relate to the world around us. The imprisonment we experience here is our inability to generate emotion and to act on that emotion (whether of desire, in the case of apathy, or compassion, in the case of indifference). And there is a grave danger in all of this, because the more we become accustomed to not experiencing emotion, the more difficult it becomes to generate any emotion at all.

One of the most telling scenes of our times is the image of an adult sitting in front of the television set and being unmoved by the scenes of pain, suffering, and horror that appear on the screen. This is the prison of indifference. An equally telling scene is that of the adult whose daily life is taken up in activities that reflect no heartfelt desires. This is the prison of apathy. Much of adult daily activity is designed to temper and mute desire. Richard Fenn's description of the seminar format in university life is reflective of much of the professional and personal lives of middle adults:

> There is virtually no single, direct statement of a personal vision that compels response. Relatively few of the speech-acts express strong feelings. . . . The expression of wishes is muted, and feelings or ideas are rather blandly reported. Indeed relatively few speakers respond directly to what others have said.[22]

Fenn says that what is missing here is the language of "real desire." Speakers talk, but they do not communicate what they really desire or long for, what they truly want to happen. Thus, if the television set is the symbol of indifference, the seminar room (and its various mutations, e.g., conference room, committee meeting, etc.) is the symbol, if not the actual breeding ground, of apathy. Both are symbols of personal bondage, because both encourage the muting and even the denial of genuine emotion.

Whereas *acedia* is primarily rooted in personal bondage, melancholy is most deeply grounded in *isolation*. This is because it rejects what it previously embraced, replacing love with hatefulness, and comradeship with enmity. Often melancholy is precipitated by a deep sense of isolation that it then continues to foster and intensify instead of ameliorate and soften. In its more extreme forms, melancholy is thoroughly world rejecting and thus renders the individual a total isolate. The fact that melancholy is deeply rooted in the sin of isolation or estrangement is so self-evident, however, that we might fail to recognize that melancholy is also rooted in the sins of personal bondage and rebellion. When melancholy turns its hatred and contempt against the self, it manifests the sin of *personal bondage*. It makes any form of self-affirmation difficult to sustain. And when melancholy takes its pain of loss out on substitute objects, it reflects the sin of *rebellion*. This is not the rebellion of pride, which refuses to recognize the legitimate authority of other persons and institutions. Rather, it is a more subtle form of rebellion, one that creates disorder in human relationships because its aggressions are misdirected.

What is most distinctive about the sins of *acedia* and melancholy is that they draw our attention to the demoralizing effects of sin on the human spirit. When we say that the eight sins are deadly, we mean that they are capable of killing the human spirit, of leaving us dispirited and lifeless. These two sins are powerful examples of the deadening effect of the deadly sins. All the deadly sins are destructive, but these two sins provide the most dramatic evidence of the deadly sins' effects on their victims, that is, on those who have become apathetic or indifferent, and melancholic. The sin of *acedia* leaves its victims empty and desireless, the walking dead. The sin of melancholy leaves its victims contemptuous of life and wishing they were dead. Because the two sins dramatize the debilitating and disintegrating effects of sin, they enable us to see that sin is like a cancer that destroys the inner structures of our lives without our knowing or awareness. If this is indeed what sin is, it is self-evident that we need powerful counteractive agents to contain its growth and confront its disintegrative force. In the next chapter, we will begin to consider counteractive measures—the saving virtues.

PART TWO

THE SAVING
VIRTUES

CHAPTER SIX

~~~~~~

The Virtues of Infancy
and Early Childhood

If the deadly sins are dynamically rooted in the life-cycle stages, we can only conclude that they are developmentally inevitable. The only way that we might conceivably avoid an encounter with one of the deadly sins is to die before we reach that stage in life. Yet we need to keep in mind that a sin is not confined to its assigned developmental stage. Thus premature death does not guarantee that the sins of later stages will be avoided. And virtually from birth we are engaged in the struggle against at least one deadly sin.

Premature death is no real answer to the threat of the deadly sins. What the Christian tradition has advocated instead is the cultivation of resources capable of holding the deadly sins at bay. Few Christians have believed that the deadly sins can be completely overcome. Indeed, the schema presented here would suggest that the battle gets increasingly difficult as we grow older, because our sin repertoire is continually expanding. But we are not without resources for confronting the sins, and it is therefore not inevitable that the deadly sins will gain the upper hand and take control of our lives. We can defend ourselves against the sins, and we can gain the victory.

The resources I will be drawing attention to in this study are the virtues that Erikson identifies with the eight stages of the life cycle. In this and the next three chapters, I hope to demonstrate that there are very powerful resources against the deadly sins. For each of the deadly sins, there is one (or more) virtue capable of subduing the sin and enabling us to gain a victory. The purpose of the discussion of saving virtues is to identify which virtues confront which sins. In our concern to combat the deadly sins, it helps to know the resources we possess and how they can most effectively be used.

The Traditional Classification of Virtues

The monks and other scholars responsible for classifying the deadly sins also worked at classifying the corresponding virtues. They reasoned that although the encounter with the deadly sins may be inevitable, we do not need to go into this encounter unarmed. The virtues are like a warrior's armor and weaponry. At worst they blunt the blows of the deadly sins. At best they decisively defeat the enemy. One of the most popular classifications is found in "The Parson's Tale" in Chaucer's *Canterbury Tales*. Here, Chaucer identifies a virtue or set of virtues for each of the deadly sins:

Deadly Sins	*Virtues*
Gluttony	Abstinence, temperance, sobriety
Anger	Patience
Greed	Mercy
Envy	Love of God, neighbor, and enemy
Pride	Humility
Lust	Chastity, continence
Acedia and sloth	Fortitude

Since Chaucer's list includes only seven deadly sins, he proposes no virtue to correspond to the sin of melancholy.

We could perhaps make use of Chaucer's list of virtues. But Erikson has also developed a schedule of virtues to correspond to his eight stages of the life cycle. I consider this a more useful model than Chaucer's, for two reasons. First, Chaucer's list of virtues tends to emphasize *avoidance* of sin through self-control or self-denial. This is especially true of his virtues of abstinence, patience, humility, and chastity, and is partially true of fortitude. I prefer to view virtue in more active terms. One of the dictionary definitions of virtue describes it as an "effective power or force; efficacy; potency; especially, the ability to heal or strengthen, as the virtue of a medicine." If we view the deadly sins as genuinely deadly—as malevolent powers—it follows that the virtues, to be saving, must show greater agency than do those on Chaucer's list.

Second, Erikson's schedule of virtues is based on his dynamic understanding of the life stages. Thus he views virtue as a vital strength that issues out of an effective negotiation of the crisis of a given stage. His schedule enables us, therefore, to link the deadly sin and the saving virtue of a given stage dynamically. Both are rooted in the same dynamic. Because of the dynamic they share, the sin and the virtue of a given stage bear a dialectical relation to each other. The implications of this second point will be developed later in this chapter and the two following chapters, when I illustrate with biblical examples the connections between deadly sins and saving virtues, showing that the dialectic is often the core of a person's moral and spiritual struggles.

Erikson's Schedule of Virtues

Erikson's schedule of virtues appears in his essay "Human Strength and the Cycle of Generations."[1] He begins the essay with the observation that the "psychoanalyst has good reason to show restraint in speaking about human virtue" because "in doing so lightly he could be suspected of ignoring the evidential burden of his daily observations." Yet Erikson says that the time is ripe for a consideration of human virtue because recent psychoanalytic discussions of "ego strengths" suggest that the "human strength" called virtue might also be reconsidered. We are now in a position to view virtue not "in the sense of nobility and rectitude as cultivated by moralities, but in the sense of 'inherent strength.'" He suggests that psychoanalysts have developed an "unofficial" image of the strengths inherent in the individual life cycle and the sequence of generations. That image is functioning implicitly when an analyst declares that a given patient has "really improved." Yet Erikson laments the fact that there has not been any systematic discussion of such human strengths. He wants to initiate a discussion, by naming the virtues that correspond to the life-cycle stages.[2]

Erikson uses the term "virtue" for these "inherent strengths" because this word serves to make a point. Among the various meanings of the word "virtue," he chooses the Old English meaning of virtue as inherent strength or active quality. In medieval times, the word was used to describe the potency of well-preserved medicines and liquors. Therefore, it was used interchangeably with the word "spirit." With the understanding of virtue as potency and spirit, the question becomes, What virtue "goes out" of a human being when the ego strength of a particular stage is lost or inhibited? And what are the human strengths that give a life an animated or spirited quality without which our "moralities would become mere moralism and our ethics feeble goodness?"[3]

In naming these basic virtues, Erikson prefers to use the everyday words of living language instead of making up new words from Latin roots. He acknowledges that the result is some loss of precision, because everyday words have countless connotations, but he believes that everyday words come closer to the actual phenomena being identified, and he notes that they have been ripened in the usage of generations. He proposes *hope, will, purpose,* and *competence* as the virtues developed in childhood; *fidelity* as the adolescent virtue; and *love, care,* and *wisdom* as the central virtues of adulthood.

Because the virtues are named using everyday words, I suggest that we familiarize ourselves with the dictionary meanings of the words before considering the virtues' relationships to specific life stages. With three of Erikson's virtues—will, purpose, and competence—I also suggest that we add companion virtues to emphasize that the virtues are persisting attitudes or dispositions, not single actions or behaviors, and that the virtues are moral and spiritual as well as psychological. The companion virtues that I propose are *courage* (for will), *dedication* (for purpose), and *discipline* (for competence). Here are the basic definitions of each virtue:

Hope: A feeling that what is wanted will happen; desire accompanied by anticipation or expectation.

Will: The power of self-direction or self-control. *Courage:* The attitude or response of facing and dealing with anything recognized as dangerous, difficult, or painful, instead of withdrawing from it.

Purpose: An aim, intention, resolution, or plan; an act carried out with determination or deliberateness. *Dedication:* The act of setting apart or aside for a special purpose; devoted attention to a particular object, activity, or duty.

Competence: Ability, skill, fitness; capability. *Discipline:* The result of training that develops self-control, character, orderliness, and efficiency.

Fidelity: A faithful devotion to one's obligations or vows; loyalty; faithfulness.

Love: A strong affection for, or attachment or devotion to, persons or objects.

Care: Deep concern or solicitude; the assuming of responsibility for other persons by looking after and attending to their needs; the feeling of affection for another.

Wisdom: The power of judging rightly and following the soundest course of action, based on knowledge, experience, or understanding.

Erikson's assignment of these virtues to the life-cycle stages captures how each virtue is central to the stage assigned, in the sense of reflecting its dynamics. But the virtues are certainly not confined to their stages. On the contrary, they may become even more vital when combined with other strengths that come to fruition in other stages. But it also happens that a virtue may lose its enlivening power as time goes on, as it becomes routine or ineffectual. Table 2 displays Erikson's assignment of virtues to life-cycle stages.

In discussing each virtue, I will briefly summarize what Erikson has to say about the virtue and then indicate how the virtue relates to the deadly sin to which it is dynamically linked. I will illustrate each deadly sin—saving virtue dialectic with a biblical illustration, centering on a biblical figure whose story reflects the dialectic. I have chosen to focus on Old Testament figures, and more specifically, on Old Testament males. Though certain Old Testament women (e.g., Rebecca, Hagar, Miriam) may illustrate the dialectic of deadly sin and saving virtue, the focus on men will enable us to address Mary Daly's contention that men make virtues out of the deadly sins. I do not question the general truth of Daly's argument or of her claim that men often view the deadly sins in very distorted ways. But in the biblical narratives that we will be considering, the deadly sins are neither glorified nor excused. They are portrayed for what they are: the cause of personal tragedy, the destroyer of human relationships, and an offense against God. Thus in the Bible at least, the deadly sins are not romanticized or trivialized. They are considered morally and spiritually dangerous. Men who are in the deadly grip of one or more of the sins are portrayed as tragic and desperate—men whose lives are truly lamentable.

In this chapter, I will discuss the virtues of the first two life-cycle stages. The virtues of three additional stages will be discussed in each of the two following chapters.

The Saving Virtue of Hope

Erikson assigns hope to the infancy stage. He describes hope as the "enduring belief in the attainability of fervent wishes, in spite of the dark urges and rages which mark the beginning of existence."[4] Such hope is verified by a combination of experiences in the infant's "prehistoric" era, before speech and verbal memory develop. The experiences involve interaction with a "care-taking person" who responds to our physical and emotional needs and whom we therefore endow with trust. From these experiences, hope emerges as a basic quality of our existence, an attitude or disposition toward life that remains with us even when specific hopes are not met. We recognize its indepen-

TABLE 2: ERIKSON'S LIFE-CYCLE STAGES AND THE SAVING VIRTUES

Stage							
Mature adulthood							Wisdom
Adulthood						Care	
Young adulthood					Love		
Adolescence				Fidelity			
School age			Competence (and discipline)				
Play age		Purpose (and dedication)					
Early childhood	Will (and courage)						
Infancy	Hope						

dent reality in instances where a specific hoped-for event has already been quietly superseded by a more advanced set of hopes. We do not wait for the verification of one hope before entertaining another.

As we grow, we become more discriminating in where to place our hopes and what to hope for. We develop a greater capacity for renunciation and an increased ability to transfer disappointed hopes to better prospects. We also learn to dream what is imaginable and to focus our expectations on what would appear to be possible. In this way hope maintains itself in the face of disappointment and adapts its desires to what is realizable. This is not to say that it reduces desire to what is merely realistic, or automatic. For even as faith is said to move mountains, hope "proves itself able to change facts." Hope makes a difference in the outcome of events.

Erikson emphasizes the crucial role of trust, especially trust in a caring person, in evoking and sustaining hope. In turn, he stresses the importance of hope for the very survival of the infant. Our questions are, What is the dynamic relationship between gluttony and hope? and, How is hope able to confront gluttony and overcome it?

Gluttony and hope are both rooted in the dynamics of basic trust versus basic mistrust. Hope is grounded in basic trust, in trust that the world is essentially reliable. Without such confidence, there is no basis for anticipating that our desires will be met. Gluttony, on the other hand, is grounded in mistrust and indiscriminate trust. Gluttony reflects a mistrust of the future. It reflects an inability to develop a hopeful attitude or disposition that is independent of specific concrete desires. It focuses on the present moment of need gratification and dares not look beyond this moment. Infants who need to manipulate the environment by forcing the caring person to appear on demand and by clamoring for food even when they are not hungry epitomize the desperate and hopeless nature of gluttony.

Gluttony also reflects indiscriminate trust. The gluttonous are insufficiently suspicious of harmful substances and too willing to trust that these things will not cause irreparable harm. Their indiscriminate trust produces a kind of fantasy thinking that we may call indiscriminate hope. Indiscriminate hope does not take the real world and its dangers into account, whereas real hope involves the training of expectations so that they are responsive to the real world and not oblivious of its dangers and threats. Discriminating hope is imaginative but not foolhardy. Unlike gluttony, it knows how to limit and channel its desires. It also knows that there is a tomorrow and that what we take into our bodies (and minds) can in fact impair our engagement with the world later. Gluttony is oblivious of tomorrow, seeking whatever gratification can be obtained today and paying no regard to what harm it may cause later. Genuine, discriminating hope combats this attitude by evoking an anticipation of tomorrow, a tomorrow in which heartfelt desires will continue to be met and sensible living today will be rewarded.

Thus both gluttony and hope are grounded in the dynamics of basic trust versus basic mistrust, but gluttony comes down on the side of mistrust and excessive trust, whereas hope is fueled by a discriminating trust. A hopeful attitude toward life quietly but insistently rejects whatever claims gluttony makes for itself and whatever rationalizations it offers in its own behalf. Hope looks to the future and its possibilities. In this light, gluttony's concern for immediate gratification and its unconcern for the future are revealed to be not only terribly shortsighted but self-destructive as well.

Esau: Oblivious and Unaware

A biblical example of the gluttony-hope dialectic is found in Esau. Two episodes relating to his birthright involve food. In the first episode, he sold his birthright for some lentil soup and bread, choosing immediate gratification over a much more desirable but future goal. In the second episode, he prepared his father a wonderful meal, oblivious of the fact that as he was doing so, he was being tricked out of his birthright by his brother and mother. In the first instance, he took what he could get now because he had no confidence in the future. In the second instance, he was overly trusting and caught unawares by the treachery of others. The spirit of gluttony, with its mistrust and its indiscriminate trust, characterizes the young Esau. His preoccupation with food and its immediate concrete satisfactions caused him to lose sight of, and to lose out on, the more advanced set of desires and hopes represented by the birthright. In a certain sense the birthright he relinquished was hope itself.

On the other hand, the mature Esau is portrayed as a man who did not lament the loss of his birthright but set his hopes on what was still possible for him to realize. By the time he had his famous reunion with his brother Jacob, he had made up for his loss and was not revengeful toward his brother. We do not know what was responsible for the change in him, but his behavior in the reunion suggests that gluttony was no longer the dominant orientation of his life and that he had found grounds for a hopeful outlook based on genuine trust.

Chaucer's parson says that the virtues for counteracting gluttony are abstinence, temperance, and sobriety. But these are inadequate for confronting gluttony, for two reasons. One is that they are largely behavioral and have nothing to say about the attitudes or dispositions that give rise to gluttony. They are strategies for dealing with gluttony, but they are not in themselves virtues in the sense of inherent strengths. They tell us to do something or, more frequently, to stop doing something, but the injunctions are not grounded in a change in our whole orientation to life. The second reason is that the behaviors recommended are primarily based on the avoidance of certain activities—doing by not doing—and therefore fail to envision a new way of engaging the world. In contrast, hope is not merely a form of behavior. It is a personal disposition, an attitude toward life, and therefore it survives temporary disappointments and frustrations of desires. What is more, it gives rise to active engagement with the world. It replaces gluttonous actions with a whole new set of behaviors that are possible only when our basic attitude toward life has become hopeful.

There is no denying that abstinence, temperance, and sobriety may play a role in our struggle against gluttony. By terminating our gluttonous behavior, we are setting the stage for a significant attitudinal change. But avoiding gluttonous behavior through abstinence, temperance, and sobriety does not get to the root cause of our behavior, which is mistrust and indiscriminate trust. Only when the root cause is addressed and grounds for genuine trust are discovered and activated will we be armed with an effective weapon against gluttony.

Thus Erikson's assignment of hope to the first developmental stage draws attention to the fact that the real opponent of gluttony is hope. Hope envisions the possible, it changes facts about ourselves and the world, it is not overwhelmed by disappointment, and it knows how to limit and channel its desires without relinquishing them. Hope is therefore a powerful weapon in the struggle against gluttony. Or to put it another way, gluttony's greatest support is hopelessness. In fact, in the final analysis hopelessness is what gluttony feeds upon.

The Saving Virtues of Will and Courage

As infants we hope for the realization of our desires. As children in the next stage of life, we actively pursue our interests. In this, the stage of autonomy versus shame and doubt, we rapidly acquire the physical and cognitive capacities—including awareness, attention, manipulation, verbalization, and locomotion—that enable us to act on our own desires. At the same time our freedom to act is limited. We learn that we are subject to the control of others and that we need to exercise self-control. And this is where the major virtue for this stage—will —comes in. Will is both the determination to act on our desires and the acceptance of the fact that our freedom to act is not unlimited.

Erikson says that "to will does not mean to be willful, but rather to gain gradually the power of increased judgment and decision in the application of drive."[5] Will involves free choice, but it also means exercising self-restraint as we recognize that we do not have total freedom to act as we would like. We exercise self-restraint when, for example, we accept the fact that some of our goals do not really seem worth despairing over and we voluntarily control or limit our aims. The virtue of will, then, reflects a spirit of cooperation. As a virtue, an inherent strength, will involves a willingness that is activated without "having to be told," and it involves a good will in which a potential battle of wills between ourselves and some other person who threatens to control us is averted through a mutual limitation of freedom and control. (Gandhi's efforts against the mill owners during India's struggle for independence afford an excellent example of how "good will" may prevail in what could easily turn into a violent confrontation.)[6] When we have a will, and are not merely being willful, we are able to determine what desires are essential for maintaining our perception of ourselves as persons who are free to make choices and pursue our goals. Other desires, which are not essential in this sense, become matters of judicious self-restraint.

I have grafted courage onto the virtue of will because it draws attention to the fact that in the second stage of life, we experience the world as dangerous, difficult, and painful. Learning to walk, for example, is a difficult and often painful experience. The pain we experience is often physical, as when we are hurt by falling or colliding against immovable objects. It is also psychological, and thus spiritual as well, as when we experience the shame of personal failure or loss of face. In such circumstances, a decision to withdraw from further engagement with the world would be understandable. But courage emerges as a strength in this stage, encouraging us to face and to continue to engage the world in spite of its capacity to inflict pain and to evoke fears. The caring persons in our lives encourage reengagement with the world after we have experienced the pain of failure or defeat. They help us see that though we hurt, we are going to be all right, and thus they dispel our doubts. The virtue of courage revives our flagging will by stressing the necessity of engaging the world in spite of its capacity to hurt.

How is the deadly sin of anger related to the saving virtues of will and courage? Anger is our most common reaction to having our wills challenged or curbed by others. Anger is also our most common reaction to the experience of confronting an unrelenting environment, especially one that causes injury to our basic sense of self-worth or personal dignity.

The Latin word for anger, *angustus,* means narrow, tight, or constricted. Thus, anger is a reaction against the narrowing or constricting of our freedom to act at will or to carry out our wills. To react against such constriction is in part an act of self-affirmation. To be a self is to be free to express one's will. But there is also a sense in which anger is self-destructive. It is self-destructive when it does not reflect a judicious self-restraint, as when it lashes out against the other in blind fury. It is self-destructive when it causes us to retreat from the scene of our pain and humiliation in a spirit of helpless internalized rage. Here anger reveals our inability to exercise the "power of increased judgment and decision," the inability to impose our own restraints on our behavior, or an inclination toward overrestraint. It reflects a failure to assess carefully our own desires and interests in order to determine whether it might not be that some wants are not worth despairing over but that other desires are so important that we dare not give in to initial failure. Where anger prevails, such assessments and judgments are difficult to muster.

The virtue of will confronts anger by introducing an element of judicious self-restraint and a spirit of cooperation, thus averting a battle of wills from which both parties have much to lose and little ultimately to gain. Self-restraint and cooperation do not require that we meekly submit to others, accepting their superior power and acquiescing in their intention to impose their will upon us. Instead it means that we seek ways to express our wills in a constructive manner, enabling us to avoid a battle of wills that is likely to be painful for both parties and ultimately self-defeating. Will is no less determined than anger, and no less passionate. But it is judicious where anger is unreflective, and goal directed where anger is merely reactive. Anger expresses its frustration against the constrictions it encounters; will, on the other hand, seeks to create some breathing room, averting if possible a direct struggle of wills and making alternative responses possible.

In his parable of the judge and the importunate widow, Jesus portrays a contest of wills between a judge and a widow who demands that he award her the legacy that she claims is hers. Eventually the judge complies with her wishes, since he decides that, from his perspective, the battle is not worth winning. They reach an amicable solution not because the judge gives in, but because he exercises judicious self-restraint and, almost in spite of himself, exhibits a spirit of good will.

Anger is also combated by courage, because courage reflects a contrasting way of coping with injury to our self-esteem (e.g., as when we experience humiliation and failure). The response of anger is to erect a barrier between ourselves and the world, rejecting the efforts of others to offer support and love. The response of courage is to engage the world despite the fact that we have been hurt by it. One reason that anger is experienced as constriction is that we are restricted by the opposing wills of others. But another is that in anger we erect our own walls and wall ourselves in. When we take courage, we resist the temptation to build walls and we instead open ourselves to the world, even to the very experiences that caused our pain and anguish in the first place.

Moses: Sin's Tragedy

A biblical example of the dialectic of anger versus will and courage is found in Moses. In the biblical record, Moses is frequently portrayed as a man of anger. His angry reaction to his people's complaints of thirst prompted him to strike the rock to produce water, an action that caused him to forfeit the chance to enter the promised land. The actions Moses took in anger are viewed as sinful not because they were emotional outbursts but because they cut him off from God and from the people. Their effect was to estrange him from the people and from God. The fact that he was not allowed to enter the promised land is evidence of how deeply alienating the experiences were. Neither God nor the people abandoned Moses, but their relationship to him was never the same again. The tragedy, of course, was that Moses himself was the one who suffered for his actions; he was their ultimate victim.

On the other hand, Moses is also portrayed as a man of considerable will and courage. He demonstrated will, for example, in his leadership of his people. On many occasions, he exercised judicious self-restraint and found ways to avoid a contest of will from which neither he nor his contestants could emerge unscathed. And he courageously engaged the world in spite of its dangers, difficulties, and pain. In his confrontations with Pharaoh and the wilderness, he was the very personification of courage. At the burning bush, he wanted to avoid confrontation because he appreciated the pain and humiliation involved. But he engaged the world anyway, and he found that he could stand up to it and not be broken by it. In the end, Moses was a tragic figure, because he paid a very high price for his anger. But the tragedy is overshadowed by the life he lived. It was a life that was not confined to a narrow, tight, or constricted arena. He was a man who constantly tested the world's outer boundaries.

Chaucer's parson says that the antidote to anger is patience. Undoubtedly there is an element of patience in Erikson's virtue of will, especially when it involves the exercise of self-control. But patience is a rather negative virtue, more passive than active, and it lacks the vigorous engagement with the world that the virtues of will and courage reflect. Besides, in situations evoking anger, patience does little more than counsel restraint and acceptance and thus only serves the interests of whoever is the source or cause of our anger. To be patient often means to accept the dominating will of another. In contrast, will and courage confront the constrictions and barriers that give rise to anger. To exercise will and courage means to avert a fruitless battle of wills but not at the expense of abandoning legitimate goals. When patience is put forward as the virtue that counteracts anger, anger is being viewed as the desire to avenge ourselves against a superior force or power. But if we view anger instead as a sin that erects barriers between ourselves and the world, patience is no real answer to the problem, because it leaves the barriers standing. At best, patience becomes the ground for self-esteem among those who are completely hemmed in by walls not of their own making, who are unable to exercise any choice whatsoever.

In short, will and courage address the conditions that make for anger, doing what they can to eliminate or moderate them. The two virtues are a constructive response to situations that would otherwise evoke and perpetuate our anger.

Engaging the World

If we look at gluttony and anger, on the one hand, and hope, will, and courage, on the other, the major difference between them is the way they engage the world. Gluttony's engagement is distorted and misguided. Gluttony is at once too mistrustful of the world and indiscriminately trustful. Similarly, anger's engagement is distorted and misguided in that it leads to withdrawal from the world (in a form of internalized rage) or to an uncontrolled lashing out against it. With both sins there is great difficulty in developing a relationship of reciprocity with the world. Neither gluttony nor anger is able to relate to the world self-confidently. In contrast, the virtues of hope, will, and courage embody a positive engagement with it. Hope envisions the world with an eye toward its possibilities. Will relates to the world in a spirit of give-and-take. And courage acknowledges the world's capacity to hurt but refuses to allow this capacity to inhibit its engagement with the world. The striking differences between the sins and the virtues in their engagement with the world point to the fact that Erikson's schedule of virtues is itself world affirming. And the fact that the virtues of the first two stages reflect its world-affirming character testifies to Erikson's belief that infancy and early childhood are the stages in life when our fundamental disposition toward the world is formed and established. The contest between the sins and the virtues in the first two stages of the life cycle is nothing less than the struggle to determine whether the child will be oriented toward world-affirmation or world-negation.

Esau and Moses were no strangers to distorted and misguided engagement with the world. They were not paragons of virtue. But that is precisely the point: the biblical stories of Esau and Moses permit us to see that virtue is not just conventional rectitude and moral purity. Rather, virtue is world-affirmation in spite of experiences that would appear to justify an attitude of world-rejection.

CHAPTER SEVEN

~~~~~~

The Virtues of Childhood
and Adolescence

In Erikson's schema, the virtues of the play age and the school age are purpose and competence. I have added to purpose the virtue of dedication, and to competence the virtue of discipline. Erikson's virtue for the adolescent stage is fidelity. These virtues confront the deadly sins of greed, envy, and pride. We begin our exploration with the play age and the virtues of purpose and dedication.

The Saving Virtues of Purpose
and Dedication

In Erikson's view, purpose develops through fantasy and play. In playing, we develop a time perspective that gives direction and focus to our striving: "Play is to the child what thinking, planning and blue-printing are to the adult." Play is a "trial universe" in which the conditions are simplified and the methods are exploratory, so that our past failures can be thought through and our expectations tested.[1] Thus play provides a context for purposeful striving. Erikson acknowledges that some experts have argued that the purposefulness experienced in play is irrelevant to what we must eventually learn, namely, what things are "really for" and what their "real" purpose is. But in Erikson's view, we learn through play to "bind together" our inner experience and our outer world, and to link the past with our anticipated future. "Binding" must be learned before we can master the tools used in co-operative activities, the roles of a given community, and the purposes of a given technology. Thus children's play is the necessary foundation for all productive activity, including adult work.

Erikson gives particular attention to how purposeful play helps us disengage from fixation on the past. In play, we "play out" the past, often in disguised form. The purpose of such play is not merely to rework the past but "to master the future by anticipating it in countless variations of repetitive themes." The various role images of our elders are tried out, enabling us to find out what it feels to be like them. Play thus provides the first clear indications of our identification with others. It allows conscience to develop, for the voices and images of our elders are now internalized as an "inner voice" that threatens, punishes, warns, and praises. Where our elders exhibit consistent moral behavior, this inner voice has a chance to become consistent in its delineation of permissible action and thought, giving us an "inner freedom" that becomes the permanent legacy of the play age. Where the elders are inconsistent and arbitrary, we develop an inhibiting guilt that continually questions the validity of our purposeful striving and may eventually subvert or block it altogether. Erikson defines the virtue of purpose then as "the courage to envision and pursue valued goals uninhibited by the defeat of infantile fantasies and guilt, and by the foiling fear of punishment."[2]

I have grafted the virtue of dedication onto the virtue of purpose, because it helps us to view purposeful play as an activity that invites and merits devotion. Not all play is purposeful; some play is random and dilatory. But purposeful play involves dedication to a task "set apart" from other tasks, a task with a "special purpose." Often, purposeful play involves an uncommon devotion to the task or the objects at the focus of play, and therefore it assumes an almost sacred quality close to that of religious devotion. At times it may seem to have an obsessional character to it, but this is because, again like religious experience, it exhibits a remarkable focusing of attention and concentration of desire. So I would add the virtue of dedication to the virtue of purpose and suggest that this virtue gives purposeful activity a special quality of concentrated devotion to a task or objective.

What relates the virtues of purpose and dedication to greed? The time perspective of these virtues and the deadly sin of greed are an important basis for comparing them. Purpose and greed are similar in that they both look to the future, but they differ radically in how they perceive it. Greed wants to collapse the future into the present. What it wants it wants now, and therefore it thinks and acts impulsively. In contrast, purpose plans toward the future. It involves thinking, planning, and blueprinting so that our objectives can be refined and our

Lake In The Hills
PODIATRY

Emo Bonaminio, D.P.M.
Diplomat, American Board
of Podiatric Surgery

847.458.4600
Fax: 847.458.4602
1441 Merchant Dr.
Algonquin, IL 60102

lithpodiatry@gmail.com
LakeInTheHillsPodiatry.com

ted and clarified. Unlike greed, purpose does
orce but instead builds bridges to it. Purpose
nner and the outer world. Captive to its own
l misperceives the outer world. It does not
o account as it pursues its objectives. In con-
ear picture of the world so that our interac-
distorted. A major part of the effort to gain a
t world is to understand its own intentionali-
rt with them. With greed there is always the
world conform to our own desires, whatever
ltivates a real imagination in which our de-
he realities we confront and these realities
sires. Greed leads to the narrowing and atro-
cause it lacks the ability to perceive the ob-
t from our desires.

ive to the "inner voice." As it misperceives
sists the inner voice of conscience. It hears
whatever does not contravene or question
desires. In contrast, purpose envisions goals and objectives that do
not contradict the inner voice. This does not mean that purpose is inhibited and greed is confident and energetic. The opposite is actually
the case. Because it is able to envision the future and imagine the realization of its goals, purpose reflects an inner freedom that in turn reflects a good conscience. In contrast, greed's desire to have everything
and to have it now creates an inner turmoil that in turn reflects an un-
easy conscience. Thus, purpose is actually less inhibited than greed,
because when purpose is in control, will and conscience speak with a
common voice.

How does dedication differ from greed? If purpose and greed differ
from each other in their time perspective, with purpose being willing
to work toward its goal and greed wanting it now, dedication and
greed differ in the range of their desire. Where dedication devotes itself to a single purposeful activity, reflecting a focusing of interest and
concentration of desire, greed seems to want everything, its range of
desire being almost limitless. In greed, we become avaricious, wanting
everything in sight, but in dedication, we want the "one thing needful"
and put other desirable objects and goals out of sight and mind. Greed
has difficulty focusing on an object of its desire; its eyes dart from one
object to another. In contrast, dedication can devote itself to a single
possession or project. For the child in the play age, this may be a favor-

ite toy or game or book. For the adult, it may be a favorite task, problem, or cause. Greed, invested in the game of possessing, does not comprehend such devotion.

Balaam: Blinding Sin

A biblical figure who reflects the dialectical relationship between greed and purpose and dedication is Balaam, whose story appears in Numbers 22—24. Asked by Balak, king of Amor, to come to Moab to curse the people of Israel, Balaam at first refused, but then acquiesced when Balak increased his monetary offer. Balaam consulted with God, who functions in this story as the "inner voice," and received mixed signals as to whether he should go or not. He was told he could go, but then God became angry with him for going and placed an angel with a sword in his path. The ass on which Balaam was riding saw the angel, but Balaam did not, and Balaam struck the animal again and again for its refusal to continue down the path where the angel stood. Finally the ass complained and Balaam's eyes were opened, enabling him to see the threat that lay ahead of him. He went on with his journey and prophesied, but in behalf of the people of Israel.

Here then we have an illustration of greed that blinds a man to the reality around him and causes him to abuse the object world that stands in the way of his greedy intentions. But having come to his senses, Balaam was able to continue on his journey and to act with singleness of purpose, saying, "The word that God puts in my mouth, that must I speak" (Num. 22:38). The impulsive, vacillating, and abusive behavior of a man consumed by greed had been replaced by purposefulness. Once his eyes were opened, Balaam proceeded on his journey. It was unnecessary for him to return home or for God to continue to stand in his way, because he was now a man who would foresee the purpose of his journey and who was able to plan for what awaited him at the end of it. He now had the courage to envisage and pursue a valued goal—faithful prophecy—uninhibited by fear or guilt and possessing the inner freedom to speak what he knew to be true about the real world. He was a dedicated man, no longer influenced by a variety of motives but setting his heart on the true object of his mission, to speak the truth as he understood it.

Chaucer's parson recommends the virtue of mercy as the antidote to greed. He is obviously thinking here of employers whose greed causes them to mistreat their employees; he challenges them to treat their employees with mercy and compassion. The call for mercy recognizes that greed has its victims, and that is a very important insight into the deadly sin of greed. But the saving virtues of purpose and dedication expose the attitude behind greed and therefore confront the sin's very source. Greed is an attitude of disregard for the object world, for its desires and intentions. Greed refuses to get to know the object world in an intimate way either through purposeful encounter with it or through sustained dedication to a certain prized aspect of it. Given the attitude of disregard and distancing, it is difficult to see how greed can be combated by pleading with the greedy to have mercy on their victims. Those who are greedy do not "see" their victims (as Balaam's inability to see what was plainly before him attests), nor do they perceive that their actions in fact victimize others. The hope for those of us who are controlled by greed, and for our victims, is that our greed will be transformed into purposeful and dedicated action. This may not happen until we are confronted by an outside reality (as Balaam was) that is so personally threatening that it opens our eyes to what our greed has done to us and others.

The problem, of course, is that behavior motivated by greed can easily masquerade as purposeful and dedicated activity. Who could really tell, from external appearances alone, whether Balaam's trip to Moab was motivated by greed or by purpose? Behaviorally, greedy and purposeful actions may be impossible to differentiate. Thus it often becomes a matter for the "inner voice"—conscience—to inform us that what we claim to be purposeful, dedicated activity is in fact greed. A clue to the fact that the inner voice is speaking against us is the perception that our activities lack a sense of inner freedom, that we are becoming distracted by inner turmoil.

The Saving Virtues of Competence and Discipline

In the school age, we are introduced to methods and skills designed to enable us to accomplish tasks ever more effectively. Since the ultimate purpose of such training is to enable us to take our place in the society's "ethos of production," the school age involves developing the capacity to accept instruction from those who are more experienced than we are and to work cooperatively with our peers. In the school age, we develop a sense of competence, which eventually becomes the capacity to work effectively. As Erikson notes, ever since our "expulsion from paradise," we have been inclined to protest work as drudgery or slavery and to consider most fortunate those who seemingly can choose to work or not to work. But the fact is that we *must* learn to work, as soon as our intelligence and our capacities are ready to be put to work, so that our ego's power will not atrophy.[3]

Schooling is the process by which we form a "strong ego," and this strong ego develops from a sense of competence, the assigned virtue for this stage. Without a strong ego, we feel inferior in our equipment and in our ability to match an ever-increasing radius of manageable reality with our capacities. Competence, then, is not merely the acquisition of skills, though this is certainly involved. Rather, competence involves discovering that what "works" in the fabric of our thought and in the use of our physical coordination can be found to "work" in materials and in cooperative encounters. When this happens, we experience a "self-verification of lasting importance." The major impediment to the development of this sense of competence is inferiority, our inability to match our mental and physical capacities to the material and social worlds to which we relate. Thus Erikson defines competence as the "free exercise of dexterity and intelligence in the completion of tasks, unimpaired by infantile inferiority."[4]

I have added the virtue of discipline to the virtue of competence, because it focuses our attention on an outgrowth of competence that is of special importance in the school age. Discipline is characterized by self-control, orderliness, and efficiency. It is the necessary bridge between our emerging sense of competence and our future capacity for effective work. Our sense of competence can atrophy and not develop into effective work if our competence is not sustained by discipline. When teachers observe that a promising child failed to live up to expectations, one major reason for the failure is that an emerging sense of competence did not develop into a disciplined attitude toward life.

Teachers talk a great deal about their need to discipline their students, and about certain students who are discipline problems. An implication is that discipline is something that teachers do. Though that is one meaning of the word "discipline," I am drawing attention to another meaning, which views discipline as something that students acquire and become. In this sense, discipline is a personal strength—a virtue. As a personal strength, it has characteristics of self-control, orderliness, and efficiency—qualities such that if children possess them, they do not have to be disciplined by their teachers. When teachers identify a child as a disciplinary problem, they are usually noting that the child lacks the capacities of self-control, orderliness, and efficiency.

There is of course the danger that adults will make too much of the disciplined life and thereby weaken or even destroy the child's capacity for spontaneity, risk taking, and joyful venture. But it can also be argued that discipline is the necessary foundation for a spontaneous, venturesome, and liberated approach to life. In *Young Man Luther,* Erikson associates discipline with sensuality and fantasy, noting that the Renaissance spirit, unlike the medieval world view, "did not permit the body to be sickened with sinfulness, nor the mind to be chained to a dogma; it insisted on a full interplay of [our] senses and intuitions and the world of appearances, facts and laws."[5] Thus discipline is not a matter of subduing and controlling the emotions, thoughts, and imagination of the individual but is a kind of "disciplined sensuality" allowing a full range of perceptions, emotions, and intuitions to be tested and clarified in interaction with the material and social world.

How are competence and discipline related to envy? Envy may have negative effects on others, as when it causes us to attempt to discredit the envied person. But the major problem with envy is its effect on ourselves as it prompts us to avoid or withdraw from productive enterprises, especially those in which envied persons are already involved. Competence and discipline combat such avoidance and withdrawal. Persons with a basic sense of competence participate in productive activities and experience themselves as productive individuals, even though their competences may be less than those possessed by others involved. Like trust, a basic sense of competence appears to be a primary motivation and is therefore its own reward. Thus, for those of us who have a basic sense of competence, it does not matter that others may be more skillful or talented than we are. If we have an opportunity to demonstrate our abilities, we take this opportunity—not for acclaim or recognition but for the intrinsic satisfaction we gain from the experience of matching our mental and physical capacities to our material and social worlds.

But what of the inequalities of life, where some of us through no fault of our own are less competent than others? In such situations, a sense of our own competence may not be a sufficient weapon against envy. It is more often the case that, rather than taking satisfaction in the competence we do possess, we become bitter and resentful. But this is where the virtue of discipline comes in. When we possess a disciplined attitude or disposition toward life, we are able even in situations of gross unfairness to subdue our envy, transforming it from its more malign to its more benign form, and perhaps subduing it altogether. Competence says, "I may not be as capable as they are, but I ac-

cept that, because I value my own capabilities for what they are."
Competence infused with a spirit of discipline says, "I may not be as
capable or gifted as others, but by disciplining myself I expect in time
to become their equal."

Of course, there is the danger that such discipline may become
merely self-serving, supporting personal ambitions only. But this danger can be mitigated through the formation of groups or communities
of individuals who share the same aspirations and who agree to a disciplined life in order to realize their commonly shared goals. Such
groups are typically fueled by envy of those individuals or groups who
are more competent or blessed than they are. But there is nothing
morally wrong with such disciplined activities if they have no destructive intent or effect on those we envy, such as attempting to discredit
them. Typically, such activities lead to the mutual enrichment of the
envied and envier, whether or not this is openly acknowledged. Thus
competence and discipline are enemies of destructive forms of envy,
and discipline is especially the friend of benign forms of envy.

Saul: Unable to Cope with Envy

A biblical figure who reflects the dialectical interplay between the
deadly sin of envy and the saving virtues of competence and discipline
is Saul, whose envy of David is legendary. As David became an increasingly popular military hero, Saul's envy increased until Saul, overcome
with envy, sought ways to destroy David. As envy began to distort his
view of things, Saul began to lose sight of his own competence as a
warrior and king. Of course, given the political realities, it seems unrealistic to expect that Saul could have learned to live comfortably and
securely with the knowledge that David was evidently more competent than he. Nonetheless, he allowed his envy to get the better of him,
to the point where he was unable to carry out his own responsibilities.
He became undisciplined, unable to control his rages, and in the end,
he was on the verge of losing his mind.

Saul is a very tragic case, because we do not see in him any signs of
coping with his envy. There is little evidence of efforts to capitalize on
his own considerable competence, or to find ways that he and David
might work together in a productive enterprise, combining their
competencies for the good of the nation. Nor is there evidence that
Saul tried to develop new modes of self-discipline designed to bring
himself up to David's level of competence. Since he could not discredit David in the eyes of the people, the only thing he could do was
to attempt to eliminate David altogether. But in the process, David became stronger and Saul destroyed himself.

Chaucer's parson suggests that the antidote to envy is the love of God, neighbor, and enemy. The reasoning here is that if we genuinely love another, we will not be resentful of the other's good fortune or greater success. But how convincing is this view? Is love powerful enough to drive out envy? In the case of Saul and David, precisely the opposite occurred. Saul's initial love for David was overcome by his envy of David's superior capacities and increasing popularity. Love was no match for the deadly sin of envy, not because love is weak but because in this case it tried to do too much. It strives for a change of attitude toward the envied person so that the envy itself will dissipate.

But competence and discipline do not confront envy by seeking a changed attitude toward the envied one. Instead they address the root cause of envy, which is our own sense of inferiority. Envy feeds on our sense of being inferior to others; competence and discipline work to eliminate or at least neutralize this sense of inferiority so that it does not inhibit our participation in productive enterprises. To counsel that love is the antidote for envy is to say that there is nothing we can do about our sense of inferiority, that we have to learn to live with it. In contrast, competence and discipline say that we do not have to live with our sense of inferiority, that this is an attitude which can be changed. Thus, competence and discipline stand for the reduction and elimination of the basic cause of envy and hence reflect the conviction that envy can be combated by making it pointless and unnecessary.

The Saving Virtue of Fidelity

In adolescence our "ego balance" is endangered. This is largely due to the maturation of sexual capacities, some that may be acted upon and others that must be held in check. The result is a continual alternation between impulsive action and compulsive restraint. Yet in all of this there are clear indications that adolescents are seeking an inner coherence and a durable set of values. The human strength that develops in this stage and reflects both the search for inner coherence and lasting values is fidelity.

Describing fidelity as the "cornerstone of identity," Erikson suggests that it has the following characteristics: (1) a high sense of *duty*; (2) *truthfulness*, or sincerity and conviction; (3) *genuineness*, or authenticity; (4) *loyalty*, or "being true"; (5) *fairness*, or playing by the rules of the game; and (6) *devotion*, in the sense of a freely given but binding vow. For Erikson, the key here is the word "loyalty" and the adolescent's view that to be is to be loyal. Thus he defines fidelity as the "ability to sustain loyalties freely pledged in spite of the inevitable contradictions of value systems."[6] The ability to sustain loyalties freely pledged in spite of the costs is a crucial test of adolescents' fidelity.

But adolescents are also selective in their loyalty. They offer their loyalties and energies only to the conservation of that which feels true to them, or to the correction or destruction of that which has lost its regenerative significance.[7] Adults cannot coerce youths' loyalty. They win youths' loyalty by offering ethical and ideological frameworks that are perceived by youths to be genuine, authentic, and vital. In formulating his own schedule of virtues, Erikson has aligned himself with those adults who offer ethical rather than ideological frameworks. Noting that "ideologies take over where religion leaves off," he acknowledges that ideologies sometimes make use of the positive features of religions (i.e., their regenerative rituals and affirmative theologies). But they also employ cruel and pseudomagical techniques that exploit youths' need to demonstrate loyalty through the repudiation of others. His prototype for such ideologies is Nazism and its appeal to German youth. Against such ideologies, he contends for an ethical perspective that views all humanity as a single community. In this perspective, loyalty to specific individuals and groups is encouraged, but not if such loyalty entails the repudiation of other individuals and groups.

But to focus only on adolescents' loyalty toward adults and their ethical and ideological systems would be misleading. What is of primary importance to adolescents is loyalty between themselves. Friends must be loyal to one another, even where this involves sacrifices. The ability to be loyal and to be the recipient of another's loyalty is the vital core of the adolescent's developing self-worth. Thus for adolescents the key element of fidelity is loyalty. The other features of fidelity, including a sense of duty, devotion, authenticity, and truthfulness, are not unimportant, but they tend to presuppose certitude, singlemindedness, and clear sense of selfhood that many adolescents do not have and cannot honestly make a claim to. In contrast, loyalty is what they are prepared to test out and act upon, and their experiences with loyalty provide the basis for the subsequent development of the more settled dispositions of devotion, duty, conviction, and authenticity. Thus, for Erikson, "fidelity is the ability to sustain loyalties freely pledged in spite of the inevitable contradictions of value systems."[8]

How is fidelity related to the sin of pride? What links them dynamically? The virtue commonly associated with pride is humility. This is on the grounds that pride means having an excessively high opinion of ourselves, whereas humility means not thinking of ourselves more highly than we ought to think. But pride and fidelity are also dynamically linked and, I believe, in a more fundamental way.

The major problem with pride is its isolationism. Pride is a type of self-love or self-regard in which we deny our need for community with others. Pride may also take the form of social elitism or exclusivism, or reflect an inordinate satisfaction with our personal abilities and achievements, leading to an unwillingness to cooperate with others in a productive enterprise. Humility cannot do very much about pride's isolationism. It may encourage those of us who are prideful to accept the company of persons we consider inferior to us, but this does little to change our superior attitude. For such a change to occur, we need to acquire a new understanding of the source of our self-worth. Humility is an acknowledgement of the fact that we may not be as good or important as we think we are, but it does not of itself help us toward any new understanding of where our self-worth is grounded.

Fidelity can help in this regard, because it has a very different understanding from pride of the source of our self-worth. In contrast to pride, fidelity recognizes that our self-worth is not based on capacities or qualities we possess independently of our relationships with others. Where for pride our self-worth is based on what we perceive to be our personal gifts and abilities, for fidelity it is found in and through relationships. We recognize our own self-worth as we are affirmed and confirmed by others and thus made aware that others consider us to be persons of worth. We cannot bestow self-worth on ourselves; worth is something that can only be bestowed on us by other persons. Self-worth is sustained not by the personal perception that we are special or gifted but by evidence that others are able to make commitments to us, and we to them. To know that we are the objects of loyalty and are therefore persons to whom others have chosen to "be true" is to discover what it means to be a person of worth. Our sense of self-worth is based ultimately on the fact that other persons are able and willing to make pledges and promises to us, especially when they go as far as to pledge themselves to us "forever."

Does this mean that we have no self-worth apart from what other persons value in us? In a certain sense that is true, because self-worth is not an attribute or even a "feeling" we have about ourselves. It is a value that others attribute to us. But this does not mean that our self-worth rises and falls as friends come and go. The ultimate source of our self-worth is God—the eternal self—who has pledged to be faithful even unto the end of the world. With God as the source of our self-worth, we need not fear that we will ever become worthless persons. Nor is our self-worth ultimately dependent on the loyalty of our friends or on our subjective feelings of personal worth. Our worth is from God, and therefore, while God's loyalty actually enhances our self-esteem, our confidence in our own way of mastering experience, it undermines and destroys our grounds for self-pride.

Thus, fidelity counteracts pride by providing a different understanding of the basis for our self-worth. In so doing, it undermines the isolationism of pride. In pride, we isolate ourselves from other persons and from God, making ourselves the center of our existence. Fidelity undermines such self-centeredness by teaching us that self-worth is not something we possess as individuals but something that we bestow on one another as we demonstrate our mutual loyalty. Self-worth is based on the experience of being chosen or selected by another. This is why "dating" is important in adolescents' interpersonal relationships, and why confirmation, call, and conversion—all of which involve being chosen or selected—are important religious experiences in the adolescent era.

Jonah: The Isolated Stranger

A biblical figure who reflects the dialectic of fidelity and pride is Jonah. Jonah's pride initially led him to avoid Ninevah, a city and a people he despised. Then when he returned his pride was deeply wounded when his prediction that Ninevah would soon be destroyed was proved false and he was discredited. By the end of the story, we find him sitting by himself in total isolation, nursing his pride in a petulant complaint to God. What is missing here is any genuine evidence of loyalty, either to God, whom he runs out on, or to the people of Ninevah, whom he would rather see destroyed than saved by his warnings. There is no element of "being true" to anything or anyone, nor is there any confirmation of his self-worth by those with whom he comes into contact. He comes across to us as profoundly isolated, the stranger on the boat, the stranger in the city of Ninevah, and even the stranger to God.

At the end of the story, God tries to break through Jonah's pride, first by making him look ridiculous as the tree he is seated under withers away, and then by teaching him a lesson in fidelity. God is perhaps no more impressed with Ninevah's abrupt turnabout than Jonah is, and neither does God have a high opinion of Ninevah (whose inhabitants "do not know their right hand from their left"). But unlike Jonah, God demonstrates loyalty. God makes a pledge to the city and its inhabitants and suggests that Jonah might also find it in his heart to make a similar pledge. We are not told whether Jonah was finally able to swallow his pride enough to see the virtue of fidelity. We do not know whether he ever came to recognize that the genuineness of prophets' words and the conviction with which they say them are directly linked to their capacity for loyalty to those to whom they speak.

Following the tradition, Chaucer's parson sees humility as the antidote to pride. By linking fidelity with pride, I have challenged the parson's traditional pairing (though I recognize that one of the virtues that branches off from fidelity may be humility). As indicated, I challenge the tradition because humility does not address the basic problem with pride, that is, its tendency to isolate us from others. If humility is genuine and not false, it may convince us that we have no real basis for elevating ourselves above everyone else. But it does not enable us to overcome our isolation from the world around us. Fidelity, on the other hand, provides a genuine alternative to pride in the constructing of our lives. By encouraging loyalty to others, it stands for a risk-taking engagement with life which is foreign to both pride and humility. It is risk taking, because there is always the danger that our pledges of loyalty will not be reciprocated or will eventually prove to be misplaced or premature (and there can hardly be a more painful assault on our pride than such experiences). In contrast, humility may relinquish its status or position, but there is not much risk to pride involved, because humility does this on its own terms and on its own initiative. This is perhaps why humility is held under such grave suspicion and why even genuine acts of humility are often judged to be false or to have ulterior motives.

Continuity, Constancy, and Moral Selfhood

If the virtues we considered in the previous chapter (hope, will, and courage) drew our attention to the world-engaging nature of the saving virtues, the virtues discussed in this chapter (purpose, dedication, competence, discipline, and fidelity) focus our attention on the continuity and constancy that characterize the life of virtue. From the third through the fifth stages of the life cycle, we are developing the capacity for continuity in our thoughts and actions. Through purposeful attention to engaging activities, through competent and disciplined engagement in productive enterprises, and through loyalty to others, we are learning to view our lives as an ongoing process and not as discrete and isolated experiences. As we progress through these stages, we become increasingly capable of sustaining interest in what we are doing, and we become increasingly aware of ourselves as having certain discernible traits, capacities, and interests. We experience the third, fourth, and fifth stages of life, unlike the first two stages, as continuous with what has gone before and what will come after. In short, we are increasingly aware of the continuities of our lives.

Constancy is also involved, because in these stages we are learning to give sustained attention to a task (third stage), to the development of a set of skills (fourth stage), and to one or more special friends (fifth stage). Constancy originates in the dedication of the third stage and culminates in the loyalty of the fifth. In these stages, we learn what it means to be steadfast and become aware of our desire that at least some things in life remain immutable.

The sense of being a moral self develops from the perceptions and experiences of continuity and constancy. To experience ourselves as purposeful, dedicated, competent, disciplined, and faithful is to become aware that we are moral selves. Thus the three stages we have been discussing in this chapter mark the period in life when our identity as moral selves is being formed. And as the stories of Balaam, Saul, and Jonah make abundantly clear, this is the period in life when that identity is most at risk. We sense, as we read their stories, that what is at stake is nothing less than the formation, as against the deformation, of a moral self. The divine interventions in the stories of Balaam and Jonah were largely intended to secure and foster the moral integrity of these two fledgling prophets, whereas Saul's tragic end is portrayed as that of a man whose moral deformation was so complete that he was no longer able to respond to such divine interventions.

Thus, I suggest that a disposition toward continuity and constancy undergirds the saving virtues of purpose, dedication, competence, discipline, and fidelity, and is reflected in the lives of individuals who possess these virtues. I would further suggest that where these virtues are being formed and developed, we may be assured that a moral self is coming into being. It is quite significant that the moral self is formed through development of virtues culminating in fidelity. As far as the formation of a moral self is concerned, the highest virtue is fidelity, with its high sense of duty, its truthfulness, its genuineness, its loyalty, its fairness, and its devotion. These dimensions of fidelity have their precursors in the earlier stages, with the third stage introducing the child to rudimentary experiences of duty and devotion, and the fourth introducing the child to social expectations of truthfulness, genuineness, and fairness. Thus the long process of the formation of a moral self culminates in fidelity. To be a moral person means that we are able to keep faith with others and with ourselves as well.

CHAPTER EIGHT

~~~~~~

The Virtues of Adulthood

In Erikson's schedule of virtues, love is the virtue that is central to the young-adult stage, care is the virtue of adulthood, and wisdom is the virtue of mature adulthood. In our schema, these virtues confront the deadly sins of lust, *acedia* (apathy and indifference), and melancholy. We begin our discussion with the young-adult stage and the virtue of love.

The Saving Virtue of Love

Noting that love is so much a part of all living, Erikson feels the need to explain why he has assigned it to a particular stage of the life cycle. Does not love bind together every stage? And are there not many forms of love, beginning with the infant-mother relationship in the first stage of life? That is true, but what makes love and young adulthood so central to each other is that young adulthood marks the transition from receiving to giving love. Love as it emerges in young adulthood has two aspects. The first is its selectivity. In young adulthood, we choose the person (or community) with whom we want to share life together: "The love of young adulthood is, above all, a *chosen*, an active love." The choosing affords intimacy, which is reflected in intimate acts but also in the forming of a shared identity where the two identities brought to the relationship create, in a sense, a third identity. The intimacy of a shared identity is a central meaning of love, and this is experienced for the first time in young adulthood: "While many forms of love can be shown to be at work in the formation of the vari-

101

ous virtues, it is important to realize that only graduation from adolescence permits the development of that intimacy, the selflessness of joined devotion, which anchors love in a mutual commitment."[1]

A second major aspect of love as it emerges in young adulthood is the role that it plays in subduing the antagonisms that normally develop between the sexes during this stage of life. The antagonisms are mostly due to biological differences that threaten to polarize the two sexes. During childhood, the ego strengths or virtues that develop are essentially intersexual and thus reflect what makes the two sexes similar or, at least, "less different." But the sexes *are* different, and this difference is most evident in the "divided functions of procreation." Thus, it is usually in young adulthood, when we are involved in the procreation and raising of children, that the two sexes are most aware of their differences. Love's task is to subdue the antagonisms that the sexes feel toward each other and to accentuate the ego strengths that the two sexes have in common. One very important function of love is to promote recognition of the very fact that the virtues are common to both sexes, that they cannot be divided into male and female "traits." Thus love is the virtue that challenges any attempt to allocate according to gender the basic strengths that are vital for any person's sense of being really and truly alive. Love, then, is a "mutuality of devotion forever subduing the antagonisms inherent in divided function."[2]

In emphasizing the positive strengths of love, Erikson also notes its potential dangers. Love can be "joint selfishness in the service of some territoriality, be it bed or home, village or country." Love is selective, but this selectivity can become clannish and lead to an intense adherence to a shared identity that we defend as if our life depended on it. To the extent that the identity provides us with a "certainty of orientation," our lives do depend on it. But there is a destructive side to this as well, if we react in rage when this shared identity is threatened. Such rage can cause humans "to sink to levels of sadism for which there seems to be no parallel in the animal world." We recognize such rage and its consequent acts of sadism in the defense of national and racial identities. But it also occurs in intimate relationships, as when a marriage begins to fall apart and, with it, the shared identity the marriage symbolized. Then we see the darker side of love as it turns to rage and sadistic assault.[3]

According to our schema, lust is the deadly sin of young adulthood. How then are love and lust related? Lust involves no real choice of a partner, and it surrenders our need and ability to give and receive. Lust is also asocial. On the one hand, it encourages "dyadic withdrawal," which drives out all other social linkages. On the other hand, it engages in intimate acts but is unwilling to assume responsibility for the consequences of these acts, especially where this involves the procreation of children.

Love is the mirror image of lust. Love involves selectivity, which chooses and is chosen by a partner, whereas lust makes no real choice of a partner. Love involves a mutuality of devotion in which the two separate identities of the partners are confirmed in a new shared identity; lust surrenders the need to give and receive. Love subdues the antagonisms between the sexes; lust exacerbates them. Lust does this through dyadic withdrawal, which feeds the antagonisms between the sexes because it expects the other to meet our every need, and blames the other when its expectations cannot be met. Lust also exacerbates the antagonisms between the sexes through its cruelty, especially as it inflames love's darker side of sadistic rage. In contrast, love reaches beyond this relationship, allowing the satisfactions of intimate love to energize the partners' actions and activities outside this relationship. In addition, lust is unwilling to accept responsibility for the consequences of its sexual intimacy. In fact, lust only plays at intimacy, because intimacy, according to Erikson, is "the selflessness of joined devotion, which anchors love in a mutual commitment" and "in the actuality of our responsibilities."[4] Lust resists mutual commitments and assumes no responsibility for its consequences.

It is clear that love and lust are dynamically linked but have utterly different intentionalities. The question is whether love is strong enough to combat a powerful sin like lust. Erikson's description of love as an "elusive and yet all-pervasive power" is not entirely reassuring, because it suggests that love may be such a diffuse strength that it cannot be brought effectively to bear against a highly focused sin like lust. But his definition of love as a "mutuality of devotion forever subduing the antagonisms inherent in divided function" points to a characteristic of love that he ascribes to this virtue and to no other, and in this lies its power. This is the fact that love endures "forever." Hope fades, courage flags, dedication ceases, competence is lost, fidelity fails. But love is forever. It assumes new forms but never ends. Lust is a fire that burns itself out. It lacks continuance. Love is an energy that lives through many transformations. Thus it defeats lust by outlasting it.

This does not mean, of course, that we are to accept the role of victims to someone else's lust on the grounds that eventually love will conquer lust. Such acquiescence allows submissiveness to masquerade as love and only perpetuates the deadly reign of the sin. The love that endures and outlasts lust is love that subdues the antagonisms between the sexes by challenging any attempt to allocate according to gender the basic strengths that are vital for any person's sense of being really and truly alive. Lust perpetuates the antagonisms by refusing to recognize that the victim of its actions has the right to hope, to express will and courage, to have purpose, to be competent, to experience fidelity, to care and be cared for, and to live wisely. Submitting to acts of lust in the hope that love will eventually prevail undermines the power of love, for love seeks to protect our right to all the other virtues whereas lust seeks to deprive its victims of these inherent strengths, treating its victims as less than human and less than fully alive. By depriving its victims of these inherent strengths, lust heightens the antagonisms between the sexes, treating the other sex as though it has no right to exercise these strengths even though they are inherent and, as Erikson puts it, "God-given."

Samson: Challenged Boundaries, Heightened Antagonisms

A biblical figure who illustrates the lust-love dialectic is Samson, whose story appears in Judges 13—16. Samson's troubles began when he insisted on having a Philistine woman for his wife, pleading with his parents to "get her for me" until they finally relented. A fight broke out between Samson and the male Philistines who attended the wedding party, and these adversaries subsequently murdered his wife and her father. Samson's own life was now in danger: on one occasion, he managed to avoid death by leaving a prostitute's house at midnight, thereby eluding the Gazite men who planned to capture and murder him at daybreak. Some time later he became involved with Delilah, whom the narrator tells us Samson truly loved. But she accepted a bribe from his adversaries for information that enabled them to capture him, and he was imprisoned. Then the Philistines brought Samson out during the great feast to their god. They chained him to a pillar of the temple, intending to make a spectacle of him, the "ravager of our country." Instead Samson seized this opportunity for final revenge against his enemies, leaning his weight against the pillars of the temple until it came crashing down, killing all the people who were in it, including Samson himself.

Samson's visit to the prostitute suggests that he was a man given to lust. But in his marriage and his later relationship to Delilah, he also appears to have envisioned what an intimate relationship based on selectivity could be if given half a chance to succeed. Regarding his marriage, however, there were no clear social supports for his idea of selecting a wife on the basis of personal desire, especially a wife of another race. Any prospects for genuine mutual commitment or shared identity between him and his bride were undermined by the larger social and political conflicts in which he had become embroiled. Samson was clearly out of step with established social patterns, especially in his determination to break through ethnic, racial, and religious barriers. The same was true of his relationship to Delilah: there were no social supports for this relationship to succeed. The prospects for the relationship were further undermined by the fact that Samson was a danger to anyone with whom he tried to relate. Delilah acted treacherously, but unlike Samson's wife, she survived him, by doing so.

The lack of social supports for Samson's innovative approach to intimate love was not, however, the only problem. He exacerbated these difficulties with his combative style and antagonistic attitude toward his adoptive people. His behavior reflected lust's tendency toward dyadic withdrawal, a marriage which drives out all other social linkages. And the fact that his wife and her father were murdered by Samson's adversaries shows that lust does indeed have its victims. In contrast to sins like anger and envy, which are predominantly self-destructive, lust is also destructive of the lives of those who through misfortune or misjudgment have become entangled with the lustful.

In short, Samson's life was a complex mixture of love and lust, of both selective and indiscriminate intimacy, of both prosocial and asocial behavior. But in the end love did not prevail, largely because there was no real effort to marshal its power to subdue the antagonisms between the sexes. Samson challenged existing social boundaries by taking a Philistine woman for his wife, but he made no obvious effort to challenge traditional allocations, according to gender, of the basic strengths that are vital for any person's sense of being really and truly alive. We are told that Samson loved Delilah, but the story generally depicts a man who viewed women as pawns in what was for him an even larger antagonistic struggle, his battle with the Philistines. The account of the wedding party in which he antagonized the other young men, and of his ill-fated romance with Delilah, indicates that men's very need to be the possessors of strength not only undermines their own bid for a woman's love but also threatens the woman's very survival. Later when we look at the story of Ruth, Naomi, and Boaz, we will see a very different picture, one where the basic strengths—virtues—that are vital for any person's sense of being really and truly alive are not allocated according to gender. The result in this case was not an antagonism between the sexes that led to destruction but a spirit of love between them which insured their mutual survival.

Chaucer's parson suggests that the antidote to lust is chastity and continence. Like many of his other virtues, these are virtues of avoidance and restraint and do nothing to change the underlying attitudes toward the other sex which give license to lust. In contrast, love is an active virtue that makes choices and abides by them. Moreover, love takes issue with lust by subduing the antagonisms, not the passions, between the sexes. Ironically, chastity and continence actually reflect the attitudes of the sin they are meant to combat, because chastity is a form of self-subjection and continence is a type of self-abdication. Unlike chastity, which is based on self-restriction, love actively pursues the formation of shared identities. Unlike continence, which encourages the selflessness of personal restraint, love advocates the selflessness of joined devotion. This is not to say that there is no place for self-control in matters of sexual intimacy. But, as we have seen, judicious self-restraint is a matter not of curbing our willfulness but of exhibiting a good will, reflected in a willingness that is activated without "having to be told." So neither chastity nor continence is an effective contestant against lust. Only love directly challenges the attitude that fuels lust, the idea that the basic strengths that energize our lives are allocated according to gender. Since these virtues are inherent—God given—such allocations are an offense against God.

The Saving Virtue of Care

The fact that Erikson does not assign care to the young-adult stage may seem puzzling since young adults are generally more involved than middle adults in the care of children. But when we look more closely at what care means, it is evident that it is the central human strength of middle adulthood. Young adults are mainly concerned with caring for their own children; middle adults are expected to attend to care in the whole succession of generations. Adults need to concern themselves with what the rising generation of young adults needs and aspires to as it begins to assume a more influential role in society. In reflecting on the caring role of middle adults, Erikson gives more attention to the teaching than the parental role, because teaching involves transmitting to the next generation the valued legacies and meaningful achievements of our own and earlier generations.

Thus care is most obviously present when adults engage in teaching younger generations, thereby keeping valued facts alive, professing painfully acquired truths, and representing a "particular world image and style of fellowship." Of course, such teaching is not limited to the teaching profession, the educational institution, or the formal classroom. The "teaching passion" is the responsibility and privilege of all caring adults and reflects a basic feature of all forms of care, namely, the adult's own need to be needed. Adults derive much satisfaction from explaining to younger persons what is important and from being understood by them.[5] By being needed, adults avoid succumbing to the "mental deformation of self-absorption."[6]

This suggests that care is twofold. It obviously involves the care of the younger generation itself. But because it focuses on the transmission of valued legacies and meaningful achievements of our own and previous generations, it also involves care for those legacies and achievements, and the training of the younger generation so that it is equipped to take care of them also. Thus Erikson defines care as the "widening concern for what has been generated by love, necessity, or accident," and by "widening concern" he means care that potentially extends to whatever a given generation creates and leaves behind.[7] A major part of this widening concern is for the adult generation to assess the consequences of what it has already generated, especially consequences that it did not intend and that may no longer be within its power to control. On the national and international level, there is included a concern for our production of destructive weapons. On the more personal level, there is a concern for the consequences of our earlier actions and decisions, and the attempt either to bring the earlier initiatives to greater fulfillment or to assess the damage our earlier initiatives may be causing and to take steps to reduce or eliminate their destructive effects.

What is the link between care and *acedia*? *Acedia* involves a lack of concern (indifference) and the inability to be "moved" by what is happening around us (apathy). Clearly, care is the direct antithesis of indifference and apathy. Care is a widening concern for what has been generated; indifference is a lack of concern, including a lack of concern for the unintended consequences of our generativity. Care has its basis in the need to be needed; apathy is a condition in which we are dead to all personal needs, including the need to be needed by others. Apathetic persons do not feel needed: "The world will continue to survive without me," and, "If I disappeared from the face of the earth today, no one would notice."

The question, then, is not whether care is dialectically linked to *ace-*

dia but how persons who have become care-less can learn to care again and how those who feel they are beginning to succumb to apathy or indifference may turn the tide against this dangerous trend. Indifference and apathy cannot be overcome simply by a conscious act of will. To say, "I am determined to care," is a heroic gesture, but it is difficult to bring oneself to care without inspiration from others. One source of inspiration is the younger generation itself. Younger persons do middle adults a great service when they "demand" to be taught and thereby stimulate the older persons' need to be needed, helping them fend off the mental deformation of self-absorption. Unfortunately it is the rare adolescent or young adult who, in observing that a middle adult has become indifferent and apathetic, will take deliberate steps to inspire the adult to care again. And those who do take such steps often find that rather than inspiring the indifferent or apathetic adult, they are instead drawn into the adult's pathology and incur the risk of becoming cynical and despairing themselves.

Another source of inspiration is God. Erikson acknowledges that one reason we humans envision "all-caring gods" is that we have a persisting infantile need for being taken care of. But another reason is that we seek guidance in how to interpret our generative role, and forgiveness for having misinterpreted it.[8] This means that our own caring depends at least in part on our perception that God cares for the world that has been entrusted to our care. What challenges our apathy and indifference, therefore, is the awareness that God cares for the world, and thus we are obliged and privileged to care for it too. This means allowing our understanding of God's care for the world to inform our own intentions and acts.

Acedia is a sin that ultimately only God can overcome, because the recovery of care requires a spiritual renewal—being moved from within by the spirit of God. But this does not mean there is nothing we can do to foster the renewal. Heroic resolutions to care again will only lead to greater despair. But an initial step in the recovery of our capacity to care may be a simple heartfelt prayer for forgiveness for avoiding or misinterpreting our generative role. If a period of *acedia* enables us to take stock of what we in our generativity have done, then our confrontation with that deadly sin will have served a useful purpose. It will lead perhaps to a reinterpretation of what caring for the world means for us in our individual circumstances. *Acedia* exacts a heavy spiritual and psychological price. But a confrontation with *acedia* may convince us in ways no other experience could of God's own care for the world. To recover from *acedia* is to experience at first hand the depth and persistence of God's care, which leaves nothing in the world for dead.

Koheleth: A Sense of Responsibility

A biblical example of the dialectic between care and *acedia* is found in Koheleth, the imputed author of Ecclesiastes. Koheleth, or "the Preacher," points out that he has constructed a great many houses and gardens and has acquired many possessions. But now as a middle-aged man looking back on all these accomplishments, he recognizes that all of this generative activity is "vanity and a striving after wind" (2:11). Why? Mainly because strangers, the next generation, will enjoy the fruits of his labors (6:2). He takes a similar hard look at human society and concludes that it is an unhappy business, for the oppressed have no one to comfort them, the righteous perish in their righteousness, and the wicked prolong their lives in evil doing. Furthermore, that some prosper and others do not is strictly a matter of fate, not of merit or right living. The "race is not to the swift, nor the battle to the strong, nor bread to the wise, nor riches to the intelligent, nor favor to the man of skill; but time and chance happen to them all" (9:11).

To all appearances, Koheleth's life has been successful beyond all reasonable expectations. But he is becoming apathetic and indifferent about it all. He feels that what he has accomplished is of only passing worth and, in any case, his achievements will fall into the hands of the next generation, who will abuse or destroy them. He also doubts that anyone has much interest in what he has to teach, including the ideas that he is currently expressing, because he suspects that people put little stock in wisdom and he acknowledges that wisdom cannot explain the meaning of human activity and events anyway.

Yet, in spite of his indifference and apathy, Koheleth does not abandon his teaching role altogether. In Erikson's words, he "outlines a particular world image" in which he advises the younger generation to enjoy the simple pleasures of life and work for whatever intrinsic satisfactions such work affords. He also advocates the pursuit of wisdom, because wisdom, for all its inadequacies, is more to be desired than power and influence. And in spite of his suspicions about human pursuits, he reveals a deep concern for the future of the earth, noting that as human projects crumble, fall, and return to dust, the earth is thereby replenished. The earth, which is the very source of human survival, is revitalized by the very failure and fragility of human enterprises.

Koheleth's vision is sober, bordering on the cynical. But he reflects the dialectical struggle between *acedia* on the one hand and care on the other. He cites all the reasons that a middle adult would succumb to apathy and indifference, and he speaks as one who has experienced both, not once or twice but more often than he cares to remember. But he has not succumbed to the "mental deformation of self-absorption," living only to be cared for by others. What staves off this self-absorption is a sense of responsibility for what he and his generation have made of the world. He has worked, and worked hard, but it has not turned out at all as he expected. He has produced much, but he takes no delight or satisfaction in it. If he does not ask for forgiveness for the unintended consequences of his productivity, he nonetheless allows himself no illusions about their actual worth. And despite his cynical comments about the younger generation, he appears to want those whom he is teaching to cultivate a similar sense of responsibility for what they will be generating. In this sense, he believes that he and his peculiar brand of wisdom are urgently needed, even if those he teaches do not recognize their need for the wisdom or for him.

Chaucer's parson identifies the seventh deadly sin as *acedia* and sloth and proposes that the antidote to the sin is fortitude, which manifests itself in magnanimity and magnificent works of goodness. Although fortitude may be a valuable antidote for sloth, it is difficult to see how it can combat apathy or indifference. There is little reason, therefore, for us to discuss the parson's views on fortitude further. Better to end our consideration of care with the views of the more ancient preacher who understood that apathy and indifference are far more destructive than sloth, and that the maintenance of a caring attitude toward life involves more than magnanimous acts, however meritorious they may be.

The Saving Virtue of Wisdom

Erikson laments the fact that Western civilization has no real concept of the "whole of life," in the way the civilizations of the East do. Our Western world image is a "one-way street to never ending progress interrupted only by small and big catastrophes," and this means that our individual lives "come to be one-way streets to success—and sudden oblivion."[9] There is no "wholeness of life" in these images of the world and the individual self.

Nevertheless, by describing his theory as a life-cycle theory, not a life-course or life-span theory, Erikson envisions such wholeness. The potential for wholeness occurs in the eighth stage of life, when an individual life circles back to its beginnings. The very old become like children. And the critical question is whether this "return" is to a childlikeness seasoned with wisdom or to mere childishness, whether it reflects wholeness or final oblivion. For older individuals themselves, this question concerns the very integrity of their lives. The question also concerns the integrity of the society's whole way of life, because evidence that old age is a sanctioned period of childishness weakens the "vital fiber" of the younger generations: "Any span of the cycle lived without vigorous meaning, at the beginning, in the middle, or at the end, endangers the sense of life and the meaning of death in all whose life stages are intertwined."[10] In effect, the younger generation needs to be able to see wisdom personified in the older generation. Then the older generation represents "to the coming generation a living example of the 'closure' of a style of life."[11] When this occurs, the younger generation can have confidence in what the society makes of itself. When such wisdom is patently absent or of questionable value, the younger generation has good reason to despair even of its own old age.

Wisdom, of course, is not limited to the final stage of life. Younger persons can exemplify wisdom. But wisdom is the special strength of the old. Among the old, wisdom is a "detached concern with life itself, in the face of death itself."[12] The key words here are "detached concern," which Erikson clarifies by comparing wisdom to knowledge. Throughout the life cycle, individuals have been acquiring knowledge, either through their own direct experience or through the study and observation of the experience of others. But in old age, wisdom "is the essence of knowledge freed from temporal relativity."[13] Wisdom is the knowledge that envisages the whole of life, that views human problems in their entirety.

Wisdom, as the ability to envisage human problems in their entirety, requires vigor of mind and the gift of responsible renunciation. Older persons who are wise continue to give vigorous thought to human problems and their solutions. At the same time, their concern for these problems is disinterested, because they know that their own life is coming to an end and that they will probably not live long enough to gain personally from the solving of the problems. Hence wisdom is a detached concern, but this certainly does not mean that it involves an emotional withdrawal from human affairs. In one sense, our investment is even more intense because we are concerned to see human problems in a holistic way and not simply from the perspective of our own self-interest.

The greatest threat we experience to maintaining wisdom in old age is the knowledge that "a limited life is coming to a conscious conclusion."[14] This knowledge is the adversary of wisdom, and its demoralizing power cannot be overestimated. As we stand at the entrance to the valley that we must cross alone, our individuality finds "its ultimate test." Wisdom cannot expel the knowledge of our approaching death but can only hope to coexist with it.

In addressing this threat to wisdom, Erikson acknowledges that he is approaching the "psychology of 'ultimate concern,'" which he says he is not ready to discuss in any detail. Yet he admits to his "feeling" that the "order" depicted in his schedule of human virtues has an "existential complementarity" in the "great Nothingness," that is, the reality that exists beyond and perhaps encompasses the "gods of human creation and projection." His point here is that the human strengths he has outlined are also the vital forces within the very order of existence. Thus one of the functions of wisdom in old age is to view these human strengths in a more holistic way, as coterminous with the very structures of reality. In old age, we experience the virtues less in relation to the crises of particular stages and more from the perspective or vision of the "whole of life," meaning not only the life of an individual, a society, or even all humanity, but the very order of life itself.[15]

What links wisdom and melancholy? Melancholy is the deadly sin of old age, because this is when loved objects are lost and cannot be replaced. In melancholy, we turn against the lost loved objects, against ourselves, and against others whom we associate with the loved objects. Wisdom counteracts melancholy in each of its forms. Through its detached concern for life, wisdom challenges disgust for the world that we have lost and disgust turned against ourselves in the form of internalized rage. This detached concern grows out of the same realities that spawn melancholy—out of the loss of loved objects. But wisdom is a very different response to such loss. Wisdom is more closely allied with mourning and, in fact, may be viewed as the solace that mourning seeks.

As detached concern, wisdom combines vigor of mind and the gift of responsible renunciation, and together these gifts enable us to withstand the assaults of melancholy. Melancholy weakens the mind by allowing it to be filled with resentment; wisdom invigorates the mind by enabling it to view our problems, including the inevitability of loss and death, from the perspective of the "whole of life." Melancholy needs to denounce and repudiate what has been lost; wisdom sadly but lovingly relinquishes it, in a courageous act of responsible renunciation. Responsible renunciation is the gift that comes to those who mourn, a gift that melancholy cannot acknowledge or accept.

Besides confronting the negative effects of melancholy on the self, wisdom eases the burdens of those with whom the older person associates. Wisdom enables older persons to view their own problems and troubles in a more holistic manner, and "only such wholeness can transcend the petty disgust of feeling finished and passed by."[16] The sense of wholeness makes life more bearable for those who care for the old. When we attribute wisdom to the old, it is not because they are able to make impressive pronouncements of truth or meaning based on their extensive experience with human affairs. Rather their acclaimed wisdom is owing to the way they conduct themselves in their everyday dealings with others: they behave in a manner that bespeaks both a vigor of mind in spite of the inevitable loss of certain cognitive and perceptual capacities, and the gift of responsible renunciation, including acceptance of the diminishment of basic strengths developed in earlier stages of life. The melancholic represent to the coming generation a fragmented life, because melancholics are essentially at odds with themselves, viewing their inevitable losses as grounds for self-contempt. But older persons who possess the human strength of wisdom can continue to exemplify a living sense of the "whole of life" in spite of their losses and can thereby instill in younger persons a confidence in the "way of life" that both generations, with some variation, share.

Job: A Claim to Integrity

A biblical example of the dialectic between wisdom and melancholy can be seen in Job, a man whose name is now synonymous with suffering. Job's adult children were killed when a tornado leveled their house, his sheep were destroyed by fire, his camels were stolen, and Job himself was afflicted with loathsome sores all over his body. In all this, Job clung to his integrity, even after his wife issued the ultimate challenge: "Do you still hold fast to your integrity? Curse God and die" (2:9). In subsequent conversations with friends who came to console him, Job lamented his situation, expressing the wish that he might have died at birth the victim of stillbirth, a rejecting mother, or even abortion. Often he succumbs to melancholy, complaining "in the bitterness of my soul" (7:11). Over and over again, he says that he loathes his life and would choose strangling and death over the existence he now endures. It angers him that other people, even the wicked, continue to lead productive lives while he sits on his dungheap scraping himself with a chunk of pottery.

Disgust for himself and for the world nearly consumes him. It affects his attitude toward his friends, whose words of encouragement evoke bitter sarcasm: "No doubt you are the people, and wisdom will die with you" (12:2). He pleads with God, whom he blames for all his troubles: "Let me alone, that I may find a little comfort before I go whence I shall not return, to the land of gloom and deep darkness" (10:20–21). Yet in spite of his disgust for himself and the world, he does not sink to the depths of melancholy from which he cannot recover. Instead, throughout his ordeal he refuses to relinquish his claim that he has been a man of integrity. He responds angrily to his friends' view that he is being punished for some great wickedness and therefore should confess, humble himself before God, and derive blessings from this act of contrition. Instead he contends that he has lived a life of integrity and that his friends are utterly unable to cite evidence to the contrary. Furthermore, why should he repent of wicked acts he has not committed, when all the evidence indicates that God does not really care whether people are righteous or not? So to his friends he says, "Far be it from me to say that you are right; till I die I will not put away my integrity from me. . . . My heart does not reproach me for any of my days" (27:5–6).

The determination to hold on to his integrity and to do so at all costs is indicative of Job's wisdom. When God responds at last to Job, there is the scathing reminder that Job does not possess knowledge of why things happen as they do. But such knowledge is not the issue here. What counts is that Job is the very personification of wisdom as he sits on his dungheap and refuses to let his friends question the basic integrity of his life. In his conversations with friends, Job demonstrates a vigor of mind more impressive than that of his counselors. His vigor of mind enables him to maintain his integrity in spite of physical debilitation and perhaps loss of certain mental and perceptual functions as well. He contends that his life has wholeness and that such a life provides a living example for the coming generation. It is significant that God does not dispute Job's claim. On the contrary, God reprimands Job's friends for challenging his integrity and for trying to get Job to accept personal responsibility for losses that were due to circumstances beyond his control. Of course, Job's claim to integrity does not mean that he lived a perfect moral life. Integrity does not mean moral perfection. Instead it means knowing that one's life has an essential wholeness that can be vigorously defended.

Job has been a role model for others who, confronted with similar losses, have not been strangers to a melancholic disgust for themselves and the world but yet have continued to affirm the essential integrity of their lives. We are not told whether Job is an old man in the eighth stage of life or whether he is a younger man who because of misfortune is compelled to reflect on the concerns associated with old age. But he is a powerful example of the wisdom of the old. As Erikson puts it, old persons "can envisage human problems in their entirety (which is what 'integrity' means) and can represent to the coming generation a living example of the 'closure' of a style of life. Only such integrity can balance the despair of the knowledge that a limited life is coming to a conscious conclusion, only such wholeness can transcend the petty disgust of feeling finished and passed by, and the despair of facing the period of relative helplessness which marks the end as it marked the beginning."[17] The West may lack a *concept* of the whole of life, but in Job the Judeo-Christian tradition has a *living example* of such wholeness. Job's story suggests that the wholeness of life is a matter not of finding "quiet retirement" but of finding the necessary strength to confront the deadly threat of melancholy. And that means having the wisdom to see human problems, including our own, in a more holistic way, maintaining a vigor of mind and accepting the gift of responsible renunciation.

The Saving Virtues as Vital Signs

In each of the two previous chapters, we concluded our discussion of the saving virtues by seeking to identify the dispositions that underlay those virtues. The virtues of the first two life-cycle stages reflected a disposition to engage the world. The virtues of the next three stages introduced the concern for continuity and constancy, both of which are central to the formation of a moral self. As we now consider the virtues of the three final stages, I suggest that their common dispositional core is vitality. These virtues clearly illustrate Erikson's view that the virtues are vital strengths, because each of these virtues— love, care, and wisdom—is concerned with life lived to its fullest.

In contrast to lust, the virtue of love insists that all of the vital strengths that we call virtues are accessible to everyone, irrespective of the person's sex. The saving virtues we have been discussing in this book are not allocated according to gender. Nor is it the case that men are deficient in certain virtues and women in others. If such allocation were permitted and deficiencies assumed, that would be tantamount to saying that none of us are allowed to be fully and truly alive. Thus the virtue of love establishes the essential link between the saving virtues and human vitality. To be virtuous means to be alive and vital, to have spirit. And the virtue of love assumes, in principle, the accessibility of such spirit to all persons, and works toward the realization of this principle.

Similarly, the virtues of the two remaining stages of the life cycle also reflect personal vitality. Against the debilitating sins of apathy and indifference, the virtue of care is concerned with adult generativity, which, at its deepest level, means being spiritually alive. Against the life-destroying sin of melancholy, the virtue of wisdom stands for vigor of mind. Thus all three virtues share the common dispositional core of vitality. Together, they point to the fact that the wholeness toward which we are moving is not merely a matter of becoming better integrated. What is more important, wholeness has to do with vitality, with a sense of being physically, spiritually, and mentally alive. In young adulthood, we typically discover how important the physical domain, especially as it involves sexual fulfillment and procreative powers, is to our sense of being truly alive. In adulthood, we typically discover how important the spiritual domain, and the sense that the spirit of the living God is within us, is to our sense of being alive and vital. In mature adulthood, we discover how much our sense of being truly alive depends on our vigor of mind. A sense of wholeness, then, derives from the perception that all three domains are alive and vital. The saving virtues of the three adult stages are vital signs that tell us and those with whom we associate that we are alive to the world. Where love, care, and wisdom are found, life itself abounds. The roots of sin are rebellion, personal bondage, and isolation. The roots of virtue are continuity and constancy, personal vitality and engagement with the world. Thus, at root the deadly sins and the saving virtues reflect diametrically opposed orientations to life.

PART THREE

THE SAVING
GRACES

CHAPTER NINE

The Beatitudes—Elements of an Active Faith

If the saving virtues are our strongest defense against the deadly sins, it is extremely important for us to have a clear understanding of how the saving virtues get activated. How do we marshal them? How do we mobilize them against the deadly sins? Erikson's answer is that the virtues are inherent in us. Even as the deadly sins are part of our very nature, so the virtues are a part of our very being. Like the psychosocial stages themselves, the virtues are part of the preexisting ground plan of the developmental process. So given a reasonably favorable environment, the virtues will develop, more or less, on their own. It is not a matter of moral training as such but is a matter of insuring that the conditions are favorable for the development of these inherent strengths.

Does this mean that nothing can be done to nurture the virtues or to enhance their effectiveness against the deadly sins? In my judgment there are things that can be done, and such initiatives are not necessarily in the realm of moral training. We can be self-conscious about the need to develop and maintain these vital strengths, and we can avail ourselves of resources that are available for this. In this and the following chapter, I will be drawing our attention to one important resource, the Judeo-Christian tradition itself. Though many would argue that this tradition has lost much of its power to sustain individuals in their moral and spiritual struggles, there does not appear to be any other resource, whether another religious tradition, a political ideology, or an ethical system, that is any more effective. In fact, it would appear that one major feature of the Judeo-Christian tradition—its biblical world view—has as much life-changing power today as ever.

In this and the following chapter, I will be drawing on the biblical world view, making the case that it is an especially powerful resource for sustaining and enhancing the saving virtues. In drawing on the world view, I will not be focusing on its moral tradition directly. I have done this on previous occasions, noting the value of the Book of Proverbs as a moral perspective for our times. Instead I will focus on two other biblical forms, namely, the Beatitudes of Jesus and the narrative tradition (with particular emphasis on its pilgrimage motif). These are not the only biblical resources available to us. They might not even prove to be the most valuable ones for sustaining the saving virtues. But I hope to show that they are very powerful indeed, and certainly much more helpful in the long run than the moral prohibitions that we often consider to be our best weapons against the deadly sins. They are powerful because they encourage and undergird the dispositions that are fundamental to the saving virtues—engagement with the world, continuity and constancy, and vitality. In the present chapter, we will be focusing on the Beatitudes.

The Eight Beatitudes

In his article on the Galilean sayings of Jesus, Erikson notes that Jesus' sayings address and affirm the individual's propensity for an "active faith." Thus these sayings focus on our "vital core in the immediate present" instead of our "dependence on traditional promises and threats of a cosmic nature."[1] Though Erikson does not discuss the Beatitudes directly, it would be consistent with his whole line of argument to say that Jesus' beatitudes are an exhortation to such an "active faith." And like the sayings that Erikson extracts from selected healing stories ("Your faith has made you well"), the Beatitudes do not simply "talk about" faith but actually engender and empower it.

Of course, the Beatitudes are not the only biblical exhortation to active faith. Other examples include the list of the fruits of the spirit in Gal. 5:22–23 and the famous hymn on the "way of love" in 1 Corinthians 13. My reason for focusing on the Beatitudes, however, is that for most people, "the Sermon on the Mount is the essence of the Christian faith and life; and equally for most people the Beatitudes are the essence of the Sermon on the Mount. It is therefore not too much to say that the Beatitudes are the essence of the Christian way of life."[2] As the essence of the Christian faith and life, the Beatitudes provide a very powerful image of "active faith." The fact that they are words attributed to Jesus gives them special importance, since they are backed by his authority and vision.

Many authors and preachers have pointed to the fact that the word "beatitude" contains the word "attitude."[3] This leads them to point out that the Beatitudes are concerned not with behaviors that come and go but with attitudes that endure and grow ever stronger. In one sense, I have no difficulty with this view of the Beatitudes, because it is clear that they concern enduring dispositions toward life and not merely acts or behaviors. But in keeping with the language of the saving virtues and of the Beatitudes themselves, I prefer the word "spirit" to "attitude." The Beatitudes do not merely enjoin certain attitudes but embody a spirit which those of active faith are filled with, even possessed by. In the final analysis, active faith is not a set of attitudes but a way of life that reflects a distinctive spirit. The Beatitudes give us an image of the kind of spirit-filled life that Jesus envisions for us. Each beatitude contributes a distinctive element to this spirit-filled life. I will call these "faith elements." By exploring these faith elements, I will be arguing in effect that the active faith envisioned in the Beatitudes sustains and empowers the saving virtues.

Here are the Beatitudes as the Gospel of Matthew records them (5:3–10):

Blessed are the poor in spirit, for theirs is the kingdom of heaven.

Blessed are those who mourn, for they shall be comforted.

Blessed are the meek, for they shall inherit the earth.

Blessed are those who hunger and thirst for righteousness, for they shall be satisfied.

Blessed are the merciful, for they shall obtain mercy.

Blessed are the pure in heart, for they shall see God.

Blessed are the peacemakers, for they shall be called sons and daughters of God.

Blessed are those who are persecuted for righteousness' sake, for theirs is the kingdom of heaven.

Since there are eight beatitudes, I suggest that there is a beatitude for each of the stages of the life cycle. This means that the beatitude assigned to a particular stage formulates the element of active faith vital for developing and maintaining the virtue for that stage. The beatitudes for the various stages, and their corresponding virtues, are displayed in tables 3 and 4. As with the saving virtues, I am not suggesting that any of these elements of active faith are limited to the stage to which they have been assigned. But I am suggesting that the beatitude reflects the dynamics of the stage to which it has been assigned, indicating that "active faith" grows out of our encounters with these dynamics. By assigning a specific beatitude to a specific life stage, there is the danger that we will view the Beatitudes atomistically. Thus, we

TABLE 3: ERIKSON'S LIFE-CYCLE STAGES AND THE BEATITUDES

Mature adulthood	Those who mourn						
Adulthood		The merciful					
Young adulthood			The peacemakers				
Adolescence				Those who are persecuted for righteousness' sake			
School age					The poor in spirit		
Play age						Those who hunger and thirst for righteousness	
Early childhood							The meek
Infancy							The pure in heart

TABLE 4: THE BEATITUDES AND THE LIFE-CYCLE STAGES

Stages	Beatitudes	Virtues	Faith Elements
Basic trust versus basic mistrust	Blessed are the pure in heart, for they shall see God.	Hope	Spirit of expectancy
Autonomy versus shame and doubt	Blessed are the meek, for they shall inherit the earth.	Will, courage	Spirit of self-mastery
Initiative versus guilt	Blessed are those who hunger and thirst for righteousness, for they shall be satisfied.	Purpose, dedication	Spirit of equity
Industry versus inferiority	Blessed are the poor in spirit, for theirs is the kingdom of heaven.	Competence, discipline	Spirit of self-worth
Identity versus identity confusion	Blessed are those who are persecuted for righteousness' sake, for theirs is the kingdom of heaven.	Fidelity	Spirit of nonconformity
Intimacy versus isolation	Blessed are the peacemakers, for they shall be called sons and daughters of God.	Love	Spirit of peacemaking
Generativity versus stagnation	Blessed are the merciful, for they shall obtain mercy.	Care	Spirit of empathy
Integrity versus despair	Blessed are those who mourn, for they shall be comforted.	Wisdom	Spirit of longing

need to keep in mind that the Beatitudes are a system that is more than its constituent parts. As Paul Minear puts it, they "constitute a single poetic structure, each sentence shaped to parallel the others, each adding a special nuance to the whole. We should probably assume that all eight describe the same group of people and that the eight rewards portray a single condition of blessedness. When read in this way each beatitude clarifies and reinforces the others."[4]

To support my assignment of individual beatitudes to particular life-cycle stages, I make considerable use of William Barclay's exegetical interpretations of the eight beatitudes, focusing on his clarification of the meanings of their key words. I also make some use of similar exegetical insights by Myron S. Augsburger.[5] I am aware of more recent biblical scholarship on the Beatitudes.[6] But for the sake of brevity and simplicity, I have chosen to put more technical issues aside and to focus on the Beatitudes as they are understood and appropriated by most Christians, that is, as the "essence of the Christian way of life."

Stage 1: The Spirit of Expectancy

Blessed are the pure in heart, for they shall see God.

This beatitude emphasizes inner as against external or ceremonial purity. As Barclay explains, "Blessed are the pure in heart" means "Blessed are those whose thoughts and motives are absolutely unmixed, and, therefore, absolutely pure."[7] Augsburger echoes this emphasis on motives. For him, "purity of heart" means that "we are dealing with the center of our motivation, our attitudes and aspirations. This is an inner integrity of spirit, or motive." Such integrity of spirit reflects a basic trust in God based on our awareness of God's presence with us. Having this trust, the pure in heart "live above anxiety," because they have grounds for hope.[8]

This sounds very much like the dynamics of Erikson's first stage. In that stage, trust is established as we perceive the presence of a caring person. With such trust, we are able to live above the anxiety of being abandoned. We are able to see the face of the caring person as she lifts us up and calls us by name. The face-to-face encounter between the caring one and the infant is the prototype for all subsequent experiences in which we see and are seen by God. To have hope means to have had sufficient experience of the presence of God that we long to see God ever more clearly. This beatitude, then, promises the pure in heart that they will receive what they have longed for, that is, direct evidence of God's presence with them.

Purity of heart is a fundamental trust in God that has no other motive than the heartfelt desire to experience God's presence. Thus, purity of heart reflects a spirit of expectancy, and I suggest that this spirit of expectancy is the element of active faith which maintains the human strength of hope. Because the spirit is ultimately grounded in the expectation of seeing God, the vital core of hope is the pure desire to be recognized by another, and not (as it is for gluttony) an expectancy based on what the other has to give us.

As we have seen, hope is the feeling that what is wanted will in fact happen. This hope sustains the infant as she awaits the appearance of the caring person, and this hope sustains the pure in heart as they await God's appearance. In both cases, those who wait are sustained by the confidence that, even as they wait, the expected one is preparing to return and, in fact, has a personal need to do so. As Paul W. Pruyser points out,

> Hoping is based on a belief that there is *some benevolent disposition toward oneself somewhere in the universe, conveyed by a caring person.* Indeed, could it be that precisely when infantile grandiosity is beginning to wane the child begins to surmise that the mother's benevolent disposition toward him is not a whimsical act of will on her part, but a deep need built into her own motherhood and humanness? I think some mystics have been on the trail of that realization; said Angelus Silesius: "I know that without me God could not live one moment." And the poet Rilke asked: "What will you do, God, when I die?" It is of course easy to spot traces of grandiosity in such statements, but this impression can mask the person's more stunning *discovery that the creator and the created, or the universe and the solitary person, are interdependent and engaged in patterns of mutuality.*[9]

The pure in heart expect to see God, and they sense that God shares the same spirit of expectancy.

Stage 2: The Spirit of Self-Mastery

Blessed are the meek, for they shall inherit the earth.

Many people think that meekness means humility and a self-effacing demeanor. That may be what it means in everyday talk, but it is not what it means in the beatitude. In Hebrew meekness means an obedient acceptance of another's guidance, and in Greek it means to be under control. For Aristotle such control is the mean between the two extremes of recklessness and cowardice. Meekness takes the form of courage, and is best reflected in situations inviting anger. Thus Aristotle describes meekness as the "ability to bear reproaches and slights with moderation, and not to embark on revenge quickly, and not to be easily provoked to anger, but to be free from bitterness and contentiousness, having tranquility and stability in the spirit."[10] Plato views meekness as a combination of spirit and gentleness. From this, Barclay concludes that meekness reflects a spirit of self-mastery or self-control.

The view of meekness as self-mastery fits the second stage of the life cycle. Emerging from infancy, the child has acquired a will and the physical capacity to move about. Clashes of will between child and parent are relatively common and often erupt in anger. But children in this stage are also learning to exercise control over their newly discovered capacity to will and to challenge the will of others. Too much control leads to the kind of meekness our everyday talk envisions. The right amount of self-control produces the kind of meekness the beatitude envisions. The latter is a meekness of gentle spiritedness. It is not quick to be contentious, especially when provoked to anger. Instead, when reproached or slighted, it reacts in a tranquil and stable manner, with courage. The beatitude assures those who are able to exercise self-mastery that this will not render them weak and powerless. On the contrary, they are the inheritors of the earth. The meek do not allow themselves to be intimidated. At the same time, they do not find it necessary to fight to prevail on every issue, or to be constantly promoting themselves and vigilantly guarding their own self-interests. The meek are secure in themselves and do not need to do these things in order to feel empowered. Their power derives from the spirit of self-mastery, from the awareness that they are in control of themselves. I suggest that this spirit of self-mastery is the element of active faith which maintains the human strengths of will and courage. With this spirit, we avoid the extremes of reckless willfulness and cowardly inhibition.

Stage 3: The Spirit of Equity

Blessed are those who hunger and thirst for righteousness, for they shall be satisfied.

Barclay suggests that righteousness here means justice, right living, and a "right relationship" with God. Augsburger views righteousness as "doing what God requires," and he too emphasizes that "to hunger for righteousness is to want a right relationship with God." Both emphasize that this beatitude concerns those who have a longing for righteousness and whose longing is being acted upon in dedicated, purposeful actions for the realization of the kingdom of God on earth. In effect, these are persons who have made God's purposes their own. In their activities and commitments, they are especially motivated by a deep concern for equity, that all persons will be treated fairly, with consistency, and according to a common standard of evaluation. The spirit of equity opposes a double standard, where persons of a higher social and economic class receive better treatment than those of lower classes. The spirit of equity longs for the day when the kingdom of God appears on earth and challenges the inequities of this world. Those who hunger and thirst after righteousness do not have grandiose visions or ideologies. They have no blueprints for what the kingdom of God might look like. But they possess the spirit of equity, and this provides them with a clear image of righteous living and right relationships, both between themselves and between themselves and God.

The spirit of equity fits the third stage of the life cycle. In that stage, we develop the capacity to distinguish right from wrong. But more, we acquire a sensitivity to matters of fairness, consistency in the application of sanctions for bad behavior and provision of rewards for good behavior, and the use of standards and rules. For children at this stage, it is not merely a case of what is technically right and wrong but of whether the actions of other persons are just and fair. The children become critical of parents and other adults who exercise their authority in an arbitrary or whimsical way and fail to live up to accepted standards of basic fairness. They expect that sanctions and punishments will be appropriate and meted out fairly.

The spirit of equity undergirds the two saving virtues of this stage, purpose and dedication. We can see this especially in children's play. In play involving toys and other objects, children see their task to be that of setting the external world in order, giving it coherence and meaning. In play involving other children, there is a strong concern that individuals do what they are "supposed" to do to play their role faithfully and honestly. Play breaks down when there is the suspicion that "he isn't trying" or "she's cheating." This suggests that purpose and dedication are activated either by the perception that things are not right, that they are out of order, that they are discrepant, or by the determination to insure that things continue to be done right, that existing standards not be permitted to erode. To make or keep things right, to reestablish or maintain "right relationships," to set or keep things in order, is the primary concern of all purposeful play and the vital core of the spirit of equity. Thus I suggest that the spirit of equity is the element of active faith activating and maintaining the human strengths of purpose and dedication. Without that spirit and its hunger, it is very difficult to sustain any sense of the purposefulness of our

activities in the world. Without it, our activities, however well inten-
tioned, have a strong resemblance to random play. In churches, service projects not motivated by a hunger for equity often resemble the
desultory activities of children as they engage in random, half-hearted
play.

Stage 4: The Spirit of Self-Worth

Blessed are the poor in spirit, for theirs is the kingdom of heaven.

The poor in spirit are those who have no power, no prestige, and no
influence to defend themselves against the insults and assaults of the
world. They are the downtrodden and oppressed, pushed to the wall
in the competitive society of this world.[11] They are destitute in terms
of material goods, social recognition, and social status. On the other
hand, the phrase "poor in spirit" does not mean being depressed or
discouraged. Instead it means avoiding humiliation in the eyes of the
world by conducting ourselves and our affairs with quiet, unassuming
dignity. While nobodies in the eyes of the world, the poor in spirit do
not succumb to an attitude of personal worthlessness but instead possess a sense of their true worth.

This beatitude offers encouragement to those who are unacceptable
in the eyes of the world but are unwilling to accept society's condemnation as the final word. It assures them that they are indeed worthy,
because if it were otherwise, would theirs be the kingdom of heaven?
The beatitude says in effect that the final word belongs to God. Therefore those who are deemed inferior by the world should not despair
but take comfort in the fact that God finds them worthy and derive
confidence from the fact that they have not been "put down" by the
only one whose opinion of them ultimately matters.

Thus this beatitude supports a spirit of self-worth, which is virtually
the opposite of popular understandings of the phrase "poor in spirit."
This is not the self-worth, however, that is often discussed in popular
psychology. It is not personal self-confidence, self-promotion, self-
assertiveness, and the like. Rather it is the affirmation of self-worth
against the threat of social condemnation and humiliation. It is the refusal to allow the world to strip us of our essential human dignity. It is
the simple and truthful affirmation of the fact that "I am worthy in
God's sight."

The spirit of self-worth fits well with the fourth stage of the life cycle. In that stage, we are confronted with evidence of our inferiority
and with the personal humiliation and social ostracism that frequently
accompany it. Faced with the threat of social nonbeing, we may de-

velop an attitude of worthlessness and thus confirm society's negative judgment upon us. Or we may find deeper grounds for affirming our self-worth that enable us to put aside the negative judgments. I suggest that the spirit of self-worth is the element of active faith sustaining the saving virtues of competence and discipline. This beatitude points to the importance of seeing ourselves as valued by God, so that we are not captive to society's evaluation of us. The deep sense of our own worth confirmed by the beatitude's declaration that the poor in spirit have been chosen to carry out God's purposes in the world empowers our quest for meaningful competence and a personally freeing self-discipline.

Stage 5: The Spirit of Nonconformity

Blessed are those who are persecuted for righteousness' sake, for theirs is the kingdom of heaven.

According to Barclay, persecution occurs because someone dares to be different. The word used to describe Christians in the New Testament—*hagios*—not only means saintliness but also means difference: "The Christian is, therefore, a person who is fundamentally different."[12] Daring to be different often begins in the adolescent years. As Augsburger relates, "As a teenager I committed my life to the lordship of Christ and, while very imperfectly, I sought to live as a disciple. In public high school this meant declining practices some of my associates followed. Peer group pressure is hard to face."[13] This illustration, however, could be misleading if it were taken to imply that daring to be different means only the avoidance of certain immoral activities. If the beatitude is concerned with righteousness or equity, the daring to be different is based on a concern for equity—and not because we want to appear more saintly than others. The concern for equity may also lead to dissociation from certain of our peers—not, however, because we are concerned about our personal sanctity but because we oppose attitudes and actions that are unfair, abusive, or cruel to others.

This beatitude is closely related to the earlier one about those who hunger and thirst for righteousness, since both are concerned with equity. But the earlier beatitude focuses on the person who longs for equity, recognizing that this longing is often unfulfilled. In contrast, the beatitude we are concerned with here focuses on society's hostile reaction to persons who seek equity wherever injustices, double standards, and inconsistencies in meting out punishments are to be found. The beatitude encourages such people not to be intimidated by society's response. When equity is at stake, dare to be different. Do not conform to the world's ways of handling matters of equity and fairness but dare to be different—that is, dare to be a nonconformist in matters of this kind. Otherwise you silently condone inequity.

This spirit of nonconformity fits well with the fifth stage of the life cycle. That is the stage when adolescents are developing their own individuality and discovering that this may bring them into conflict with individuals and groups who do not share the same interests and values. As Augsburger's account of his high-school experience reveals, the results can be social ostracism, which produces intense pressure to conform to the world around us. But the beatitude provides encouragement for those who out of a spirit of equity refuse to conform. For adolescents this often means making themselves vulnerable to peer criticism, for a concern for equity frequently runs counter to adolescent mores, including sexual exploitation, social exclusivism, and the desire to win at all costs.

I suggest that the spirit of nonconformity is the element of active faith which sustains the virtue of fidelity. Fidelity involves many different kinds of loyalty, whether to persons, groups, causes, or special interests. But in the context of the Beatitudes, we are concerned with loyalty in matters of equity, righteousness, and justice. For the Beatitudes, loyalties maintained *in spite of* the claims of equity are misguided and wrong. Thus fidelity or faithfulness is not merely a matter of "staying with" another person or group, as though fidelity were measured by persistence or longevity. Rather fidelity means seeing that "right relationships" are maintained and are not allowed to degenerate into patterns of dominance and submission, exploitation, and emotional or physical cruelty. The spirit of nonconformity, in the service of equity, is the vital core of fidelity. Adolescents are often under pressure to violate their own sense of equity or fairness, and when they succumb to this pressure, disloyal attitudes and behavior invariably follow. The spirit of nonconformity secures fidelity through its refusal to go along with the crowd—not, however, by withdrawing from others (as in spiritual pride) but by standing for fairness and justice in human relationships even at the cost of personal unpopularity and social ostracism.

Stage 6: The Spirit of Peacemaking

Blessed are the peacemakers, for they shall be called sons and daughters of God.

The Hebrew word for peace, *shalòm,* has two primary meanings. It describes perfect welfare, serenity, prosperity, and happiness, and it suggests good personal relationships that exemplify intimacy, friendship, and uninterrupted good will. Noting these two meanings, Barclay observes, "Peace does not describe only the absence of war and strife; it describes happiness and well-being of life, and perfection of human relationships."[14] He identifies three relationships where peacemaking is involved. There is our relationship to ourselves. Many Christians have taken this beatitude to be a blessing on "those who have stilled the incredible battle which goes on in their own souls."[15] There is also our relationship to other persons, which is likely to be the sense in which Jesus' audience took the beatitude. Here, the beatitude stresses not just peaceloving (the desire for peace) or even peacekeeping (trying to avoid conflict) but peacemaking, or taking initiative in securing or achieving peace on all levels of human relationship. Then there is the relationship to God which this beatitude envisions for the peacemakers. The beatitude says that they will be called sons and daughters of God, which implies intimacy with God and, even more than this, a sharing in the very nature of God. The beatitude implies that God too is a peacemaker.

The spirit of peacemaking fits well with the sixth stage of the life cycle. That stage involves the development of intimate relationships that subdue the antagonism between the sexes and refuse to allocate the virtues according to gender. Such relationships are exercises in peacemaking, and our experiences with peacemaking in the more intimate relationships can inform all our other relationships and social interactions. Thus I suggest that young adulthood is the stage in life when our attitudes regarding peace in all its facets are being formed. At the same time this is when our commitment to peacemaking is under its most severe challenge. For lust, this stage's deadly sin, is the very antithesis of peacemaking. Lust is violent and destructive, takes advantage of the vulnerability of others, and exacerbates the antagonisms between the sexes. If lust becomes the model not just for our more intimate relationships but for all other relationships and social interactions, mistrust, acrimony, and the erecting of insuperable barriers can hardly be avoided.

Thus, I suggest that the spirit of peacemaking is the element of active faith that sustains the virtue of love. Love has a chance to develop where a spirit of peacemaking prevails. In contrast, love has little chance to form where only peaceloving and peacekeeping occur. If all that we have is peaceloving, we are unable to take the risks that true love requires. And if we concentrate all our energies on peacekeeping, we avoid the conflicts that true love entails. We can envision how necessary the spirit of peacemaking is to love in all of its forms, when we consider what lovemaking becomes apart from the spirit of peacemaking. If peacemaking is absent, lovemaking is drawn into the orbit of lust. Thus the spirit of peacemaking is the vital core of the virtue of love. For this reason the beatitude is able to claim that peacemakers become heirs of God, since God's own love reflects the spirit of peacemaking.

Stage 7: The Spirit of Empathy

Blessed are the merciful, for they shall obtain mercy.

In this beatitude, mercy (*chesedh*) means more than agreeing not to treat others with the sternness, severity, and righteous justice they deserve. Beyond this, mercy involves fidelity and steadfastness, an outgoing kindness in which we actively seek opportunities to express care and concern for another. In the Roman world of Jesus' day, slaves were subject to cruel flogging, and children were thrown out like refuse. Against this social background, Jesus proclaimed the blessedness of the merciful, or those who refrain from mistreating the weak and powerless and instead embrace them and see to their welfare. Barclay suggests that such kindness is motivated by a deep sympathy for the plight of the other person. In light of Minear's observation that the Beatitudes "all describe the same group of people," I would suggest that the motivation here is not just sympathy but empathy. Sympathy implies that the sympathizer views the plight of the other from a position of safety. Empathy implies that we are able to see ourselves in the plight of the weak and powerless, either because we too are living under duress or because we know that this may well be our fate at some future time. The beatitude does not appear to be addressed to persons for whom showing kindness was merely a matter of charity. Rather, because it promises that the merciful will themselves receive mercy, it implies that the merciful are well aware that they too are vulnerable and endangered. Thus I suggest that the mercy of which this beatitude speaks is energized by the spirit of empathy.

This spirit fits well with the seventh stage of the life cycle. That is the stage in which we normally have the power either to enhance or to make more difficult the lives of the younger or older generation. It is also the stage in life when we are most susceptible to indifference to the plight of others. We often justify our indifference on the grounds that we have our own problems to contend with and that no one seems to want to make our lives any easier either. But the beatitude confronts this attempt at self-justification and tells us that if we would be merciful to others, we will experience mercy ourselves. The challenge we face in the middle years of life is to be merciful, and this can happen only if we learn to see life from the perspective of those who are vulnerable and in need of the assistance we have the power to give.

Thus I suggest that the spirit of empathy is the element of active faith that sustains the virtue of care. Care is not just a matter of being sympathetic, of feeling pity for those less fortunate than ourselves. Rather, care is energized by the spirit of empathy that enables us to see ourselves in the situation of the other and to recognize that the other's plight is an offense against ourselves. Because the beatitude assures us that God is merciful to those who are merciful, the spirit of empathy also enables us to perceive that the other's plight is an offense against God. Through the spirit of empathy, we see the other's needs from the perspective of a deeply caring God.

Stage 8: The Spirit of Longing

Blessed are those who mourn, for they shall be comforted.

The most obvious concern of this beatitude is for those who have suffered the death of persons dear to them. For them, the beatitude provides solace even now, because it assures the grieving that in time they will be comforted. The less obvious but no less important concern of the beatitude is for people who anguish over the innocent suffering and evil powers of our world. These persons look for the time when the suffering and evil will end, when the world will again experience peace and well-being. The beatitude does not promise the end of all human suffering and evil in the world, but it does assure those who mourn for the world that they will be comforted. It promises that God will never abandon the world to the agencies of pain or to the forces of darkness and evil.

The beatitude affirms the spirit of longing—the longing for what has been lost and the desire to fill the void created by the loss. The spirit of longing is especially common in the eighth stage of life. It is almost inevitable that persons in the final stage of life will be confronted with personal bereavement. For most of us, the loss of our mate is the most painful personal loss we sustain in life, and this loss is more common in the eighth stage of life than in any previous stage. But mourning in the final stage may extend beyond personal loss and involve a total response to the world. Barclay distinguishes between *mourning for* the world and *detachment from* the world, and cites examples of detachment that actually reflect contempt for the world. Similarly, Erikson recognizes that in the eighth stage we may have such disgust and disdain for our lives that we become openly contemptuous of the world and everything in it. Yet the beatitude encourages those who mourn not to succumb to contempt for the world, not to see the world only as a place of suffering and evil. It does so not by making easy promises of future happiness but by assuring us that our comfort is not far off. As Barclay points out, "It is in sorrow that a [person] discovers the things which matter, and the things which do not matter. . . . It is in sorrow that a [person] discovers God."[16]

The spirit of longing generated by the experience of suffering and loss is the element of active faith sustaining the virtue of wisdom. Wisdom is not the fruit of an attitude of cool detachment nor of a stoical stiff-upper-lip approach to life. Rather, wisdom is formed and sustained by a deep longing within us for what we have lost and hope in some way to recover. And wisdom is sustained by a deep longing within us for the restoration of the world itself. In this sense, the Beatitudes as a whole are set in wisdom, because they are born of deep longing for the world and what it is trying to be. The spirit of longing reflected in the eighth beatitude brings the Beatitudes full circle, because the spirit of expectancy (first stage) and the spirit of longing (eighth stage) share a common anticipation of a time when all will be restored and whole, when all will be well with us once more.

An Active Faith

I believe we have succeeded in demonstrating some rather striking parallels between Erikson's life-cycle schema and the Beatitudes. What accounts for the parallels? I think it is that the two "systems" reflect a very similar outlook on the world. Jesus' beatitudes were addressed to those who constantly met with life's persecutions, humiliations, and defeats. Similarly, Erikson's life-cycle theory is not an achievement scale that tracks the steady upward progress of the successful and respected. Rather it is for those who have lived intimately with mistrust, shame, doubt, guilt, inferiority, confusion, isolation, stagnation, and despair—those for whom these are pressing realities. For such persons, both the Beatitudes and the life-cycle theory give a message of encouragement. The Beatitudes say that such persons will be satisfied, comforted, delivered. The life-cycle theory says that the persons will find grounds for hope, will develop a good will, will find purpose in life, will experience the satisfactions that come with competence, will find grounds for fidelity, the capacity to love and to care, and will become wise. Both constructs—the Beatitudes and the life-cycle theory—identify the blessed as those who have suffered but have not given up and who have not taken out their sufferings on those even more vulnerable than they. Thus the life-cycle theory is not unlike a sermon on the mount addressed to those of us who truly need a message of assurance.

By linking the individual beatitudes to individual life stages, we have also been able to identify the elements of an active faith that sustain the saving virtues. The Beatitudes are not moral prescriptions or even ethical guidelines. They are an empathic endorsement of our longing for peace and well-being in the world and they reflect an unusually acute vision of how God even now is restoring the world. I contend that the virtues are sustained by this perception or vision, because this vision undergirds an active faith. Our faith is active precisely when we share Jesus' vision of God's activity in the world, and our faith has spirit precisely when we sense that God's spirit is alive and abroad in the world.

In earlier chapters on the saving virtues, we looked at eight biblical figures whose lives reflected a dialectic between a saving virtue and a deadly sin. In this chapter, we have focused on a ninth biblical figure, Jesus of Nazareth, whose words put that dialectic in an entirely new light. To those who long for the wholeness that the saving virtues envision and empower, Jesus proclaims that such wholeness is not only a future promise but also a present reality. The deadly sins are a powerful, demoralizing, and dispiriting force spreading their curse across the land. But the Beatitudes counter the curse with words of blessing. Barclay says that the Beatitudes "set forth" a way of life. But they do more that that. They envision it, but they also empower it. So Jesus, our ninth biblical figure, offers a way of life and the grounds for its empowerment which enable us to confront the deadly sins and overcome them.

Active faith is central to this way of life. The Beatitudes characterize the active faith that enables us to confront sin and evil. They do not define faith or talk about faith in abstract or general terms but instead identify the elements of an active faith, elements constituting the very spirit of active faith. No single element of an active faith is sufficient to confront the whole array of demoralizing and dispiriting forces in the world. But together they can and do prevail over their adversaries. They are the spirits that activate and actualize the virtues, and they are in turn empowered by the spirit of God, the Strength of the Ages.

In his book *Dimensions of a New Identity* and in his article "The Galilean Sayings and the Sense of 'I,'" Erikson makes considerable use of the story of Jesus' healing of the woman with an issue of blood (Luke 8:42–48; Mark 5:25–34), quoting the King James Version, which says that Jesus knew "in himself that the virtue had gone out of him" and into her. Erikson comments,

> This story conveys themes which renew their urging presence in each age: There is the assumption of certain quantities lost and regained and with them a quality of wholeness. Jesus, too, notices that a quantity of virtue has passed from him to her—and this as she touched him, and not (according to the age-old technique) as his hand touched her. He felt her touch even in the general press that surrounded him, and this solely because her faith thus magnetically attracted some of his strength before he quite knew it. There could be no doubt, then, that it was her faith in his mission that had made her whole.[17]

In a similar way, the Beatitudes have the power to energize those who open themselves in faith to the world that the Beatitudes disclose. In the hearing of these words and the seeing of the world that they reveal to us, the virtue which is Jesus' passes from him to us. And with this transfer, we begin to experience wholeness and to know the virtues as truly saving.

CHAPTER TEN

Biblical Stories and
the Pilgrim's Way

In the previous chapter, we considered the empowering words of the Beatitudes and their ability to inspire an active faith capable of sustaining the saving virtues. In this chapter, we will continue to explore the role of active faith in sustaining the saving virtues, by focusing on another biblical genre, the narrative. In previous chapters, we have discussed biblical narratives, focusing on eight biblical figures whose life stories illustrate the conflict between the saving virtues and the deadly sins. The stories enabled us to see the tragic influences of the deadly sins and the graceful effects of the saving virtues in the lives of the eight biblical figures. In this chapter, I want to focus on the pilgrimage motif in biblical narratives, because I believe that we are greatly helped in our efforts to sustain the saving virtues against the deadly sins when we view our life as a pilgrimage. The author of the Book of Hebrews in the New Testament associates pilgrimage with persons of active faith. Thus I would argue that the pilgrimage motif, as it is developed in biblical narratives, is a valuable resource for sustaining an active faith that in turn supports the saving virtues.

In this chapter, I will first focus on the narrative structure spanning the first eight books of the Bible, from Genesis to Ruth. This will establish the pilgrimage motif and its relevance to our study's theme of sin versus salvation. Then I will develop an analysis of one of the most popular and influential narratives in the history of the Christian faith, John Bunyan's *Pilgrim's Progress*. The analysis will enable us to see how the pilgrimage motif not only generates a developmental understanding of the individual life cycle but also makes the sin-virtue dialectic its central problematic.

Pilgrimage in the Bible

This may seem contrived, but I see parallels between the first eight books of the Bible and the eight stages of the life cycle. The key to the linkage is the fact that both are concerned with pilgrimage. Consider what we might call the "metastory" that frames the first eight books of the Bible. This metastory begins in Genesis with the story of one family (Adam and Eve and their progeny, Cain and Abel) and concludes in Ruth with the story of another family (Naomi, Ruth, Boaz, and Obed, the progeny of Ruth and Boaz). The story begins with a family who, though created by God, sinned against God; this led to terrible consequences. But the story ends with the formation of another family that had much less promising beginnings but is in fact a model of the experience of salvation. Thus, the metastory beginning with Genesis and ending with Ruth is a pilgrimage from sin to salvation. The metastory follows the stages of the life cycle. Each chapter in this story—with each biblical book constituting a chapter—corresponds to a life-cycle stage, and the chapters and stages follow the same sequence. Thus the biblical metastory offers a narrative structure to undergird the life cycle, and because it does so, it is an extremely valuable resource for interpreting the story of our own lives as a pilgrimage whose central problematic is that of sin versus salvation.

To establish the linkages between biblical books and life-cycle stages, table 5 indicates a major theme for each of the eight books. Obviously these are not the only themes to be found in the books. But I suggest that they are the major themes when these books are viewed as chapters in the metastory beginning with the family of Adam and Eve and concluding with the family of Ruth and Boaz.

The pilgrimage begins with Genesis, which depicts individuals, families, and clusters of families in the process of claiming the world. They are free to claim the world, but their claim involves responsibility and risk. The pilgrimage continues with Exodus, where they are involved in the exploration of the world's boundaries. They discover that the world "out there" is frustrating and even life-threatening. In Leviticus, they have developed an appreciation for the lawfulness of the world, its continuities and regularities, and have formulated laws that prohibit association with those phenomena in the world which do not reflect its lawfulness. In Numbers, they confront "outsiders" or "aliens,"

TABLE 5: ERIKSON'S LIFE-CYCLE STAGES AND THE BIBLICAL PILGRIMAGE

Stage	Biblical Pilgrimage
Mature adulthood	Ruth: finding sanctuary
Adulthood	Judges: establishing community
Young adulthood	Joshua: gaining a foothold
Adolescence	Deuteronomy: preparing to possess the land
School age	Numbers: confronting outsiders
Play age	Leviticus: learning the world's lawfulness
Early childhood	Exodus: exploring the world's boundaries
Infancy	Genesis: claiming the world

groups that do not share their history and aspirations. In Deuteronomy, they make military and spiritual preparation to possess the land currently in the hands of the alien people, which they believe they have a right to possess. Joshua depicts them as having gained a foothold in this world, and Judges tells of their efforts to establish a community there. Ruth completes the story by depicting Israel as the place of sanctuary or refuge, not only for its own exiles (Naomi) but also for those aliens (Ruth) who share the same fate and destiny.

This brief summary of the themes of the metastory indicates that there are in fact parallels between the story of these biblical families and the life cycle. In the first stage of life, we make our initial claim on the world. In the second, we begin to explore the world and discover its boundaries. In the third, we come to understand that the world has rules and regularities that cannot be breached. In the fourth, we confront "others" who have no association with our own families and immediate neighborhood. In the fifth, we prepare to assume the responsibilities and to experience the opportunities of adulthood. In the sixth, we gain a foothold in the adult world, often in competition with older adults who want to maintain control of their domains. In the seventh, we assume responsibility for creating and maintaining workable communities, including educational settings, work places, and life-sustaining agencies and institutions. In the eighth stage, we seek, and possibly find, sanctuary through persons and agencies who help to meet our physical, psychological, and spiritual needs without depriving us of our freedom or violating our sense of dignity.

The connections between the biblical themes and the life-cycle stages could be developed in much greater detail. But what especially counts here is not any particular detail of the individual biblical narratives but the link we have been able to establish between the biblical story as metastory and the structure of the life cycle. That link enables us to claim that the Bible provides a narrative foundation for the life cycle as formulated by Erikson. And the narrative foundation in turn enables us to view the life cycle as a pilgrimage whose central problematic is that of sin versus salvation. Thus we are back to the deadly sins and saving virtues.

The Biblical Metastory, the Deadly Sins, and the Saving Virtues

I have emphasized that the biblical metastory begins with the family of Adam and Eve and concludes with the family of Ruth and Boaz. The beginning and ending have great significance for our interest in the dialectic of deadly sin and saving virtue. The narrative about Adam and Eve tells the story of how humankind became sinful. The story has often been used to determine which of the deadly sins is the root of all sin, with pride most commonly asserted to be the sin to which Adam and Eve succumbed (i.e., they wanted to replace God by making their own judgments and decisions). What matters, however, is not which deadly sin was the original one but that the story portrays our first family as having failed the moral and spiritual test that God placed before them. From that time forth, the course of human existence has been one of rebellion, bondage, and isolation.

On the other hand, the metastory does not paint a hopelessly bleak picture. It is neither cynical nor fatalistic. It tells of individuals and families who, now aware of the difference between good and evil, were able to lead virtuous lives. No story in the first eight books of the Bible provides a more impressive account of the saving effects of the virtues than the story of Ruth, Naomi, and Boaz. Possibly this threesome is intended by the storyteller to stand in stark contrast to the threesome of Adam, Eve, and the Deceiver. In any case, this is the story of three persons whose lives were saved because they exemplified the whole range of virtues, from hope to wisdom. But more specifically, it is a story that conveys the saving power of fidelity, as exemplified in the relationship between Ruth and Naomi, especially in Ruth's loyalty to Naomi; of love, as exemplified in the relationship between Ruth and Boaz, especially in their ability to form a union that overcame racial and cultural differences; and of care, as exemplified in all three individuals' concern for one another, especially in Boaz's ability to recognize his own need to be needed. And if we shift our attention from the characters to the story itself, then certainly the story is the very personification of wisdom, as it creates an image or vision of the wholeness of life.

Of course this does not mean that there are no moral ambiguities in the story or that everyone's motives were always pure and disinterested. Nor was the outcome solely of the three persons' own doing, for the story's plot line leaves us with a compelling sense of God's providence and grace. But as a story of human interaction, it tells us what can happen in the lives of individuals when their interpersonal relationships are empowered by the saving virtues. The story of Adam and Eve is a story of rebellion, bondage, and isolation. It portrays aimless wandering, futility, and estrangement. The story of Ruth, Naomi, and Boaz is a story of engagement with the world, of continuity and constancy, of vitality. The story of Adam and Eve is the story of a family of sin. The story of Ruth, Naomi, and Boaz is the story of a family of salvation, a family that, in spite of its very unpromising beginnings, discovered wholeness.

How then does the biblical narrative tradition become a resource against the deadly sins? Certainly it does not provide moral precepts or offer moral counsel. Instead it tells a story—about pilgrimage and, more specifically, pilgrimage whose central problematic is the dialectic between sin and salvation. The pilgrimage begins in the expulsion of Adam and Eve from the Garden of Eden and culminates in the fields, or perhaps on the threshing floor, of Boaz. The pilgrimage from Genesis to Ruth portrays the victory of the saving virtues over the deadly sins. And like the blessed assurances of Jesus' beatitudes, the story has the power to create the very restitution it portrays. The story of Naomi, Ruth, and Boaz is a parable that discloses a world to which we may orient our lives. It is not a matter of imitating the characters in the story but of allowing the plot of the story to shape the plot of our own life stories.

Pilgrim's Progress

John Bunyan's *Pilgrim's Progress* draws heavily on the pilgrimage motif in biblical narratives.[1] By placing the traditional pilgrimage motif in a new narrative setting, *Pilgrim's Progress* has enabled individuals to see themselves in the story and thus to view themselves as pilgrims struggling with sin on their way to salvation. But for many today, Bunyan's story has lost much of its evocative power. Its images and plot line have become too familiar, so that its images of evil no longer evoke terror and its images of salvation no longer evoke desire. By placing the story in the context of the life cycle, I hope that we may once again find the story to be a valuable spiritual resource in our own struggles against the deadly sins.

In my correlation of the Beatitudes with the life stages, there were an equal number of Beatitudes and stages. Bunyan's hero, Christian, however, has more than eight encounters with evil in the course of his journey. Still, the more prominent of his encounters can be linked rather easily to Erikson's life stages, and in the same sequence. This is testimony to the fact that the pilgrimage motif is the deep structure that underlies the life-cycle stages. The linkages are displayed in table 6.

Stage 1. The City of Destruction

Christian's journey begins from the city in which he was born, which Bunyan calls the City of Destruction. It may seem odd to char-

TABLE 6: ERIKSON'S LIFE-CYCLE STAGES AND BUNYAN'S *PILGRIM'S PROGRESS*

Stage	Location
Mature adulthood	Enchanted Ground
Adulthood	Doubting Castle
Young adulthood	Vanity Fair
Adolescence	Beautiful Castle, terrible valleys
School age	House of the Interpreter
Play age	Morality Village
Early childhood	Slough of Despond
Infancy	City of Destruction

acterize infancy as a city of destruction, but there is a deeply rooted Christian conviction that we must move beyond the "city" of our natural birth and embark on a lifelong struggle for spiritual rebirth. Christian senses that he must find some means of escape from the city where he is now living, though he has some difficulty explaining to his wife and children why he feels that way. All he knows is that his readings in a book—presumably the Bible—have given him a strong presentiment of ruin if he does not leave the City of Destruction. Thus he leaves the apparent security of his birthplace and embarks on the path that lies before him and that leads, he hopes, to salvation. His decision is a real act of trust, since he has no idea of where the path will lead or what dangers he will encounter along the way.

Stage 2. The Slough of Despond

Once underway, Christian's second test is the Slough of Despond. Here he tumbles into a miry bog, because fear has caused him to overlook the steps provided to enable travelers to walk around the pit. The Slough of Despond is dynamically similar to the crisis of the second life stage, where our first efforts to walk meet with failure and we fall, suffering humiliation and discouragement. One reason for our failure is fear, a fear that actually precipitates the failure that we most dread. The Slough of Despond is also a severely isolating experience as Christian realizes for the first time how alone he is. His profound sense of isolation corresponds to our experience in the second stage of life, when the consequences of shame and humiliation are isolation and estrangement. Suddenly Christian is deeply alone, and he experiences the world as alien and hostile.

Stage 3. Morality Village

Christian's next encounter is Morality Village, where he confronts Mr. Legality. He has looked forward to his meeting with Mr. Legality, expecting that this man will help him remove the burdens that could inhibit his progress along the way. But as he approaches Morality Village, he is joined by Evangelist, who warns him that the village is a false shortcut to the City of Zion, because Mr. Legality cannot free him of his burden: "Ye cannot be justified by the works of the law."

Morality Village, then, corresponds to the third life stage, where we develop a conscience, internalizing the voices of those who speak authoritatively in our lives. Bunyan's point here is that we cannot maintain or restore a clear conscience by living up to the law. Morality Village might appear to be the place where we can get free of our burdens, but this is not really so. Similarly, the third life-cycle stage makes us aware of our need to meet the expectations that others have of us but at the same time reveals that we cannot satisfy their expectations by following the letter of what they ask us to do or to be. Rather it is a matter of developing a spirit and spiritedness, which ultimately are not of our own making but are of the making of the spirit of the living God at work within us. The third stage of the life cycle introduces what will be a lifelong conflict between the letter of the law and the life of the spirit.

Stage 4. The Interpreter's House

Christian next comes to the house of the Interpreter, who through object lessons and enacted parables teaches Christian what he will need to know for his journey. He introduces Christian to two small children, Passion and Patience, who are staying at the Interpreter's house. Passion is very discontented because he wants everything now; Patience, however, is willing to wait for the better things to come. Christian learns from this living parable that Patience has the "best wisdom," because the things close at hand are ephemeral and the things for which we wait are substantial and enduring. Christian is also introduced to a man in an iron cage who cannot repent of his sins. That terrible sight prompts Christian to pray that God will help him to watch and be sober and to shun the sins that are the cause of the caged man's misery. With various lessons and parables of this nature, the Interpreter provides Christian his schooling in the Christian faith.

Christian's sojourn in the Interpreter's house clearly fits the fourth life stage, the school age. Through the Interpreter, Christian is introduced to the dangers and opportunities that lie ahead. But more than this, he is taught the method of interpretation itself, as the Interpreter guides him in his efforts to understand the meaning of the object lessons and parables presented to him. Thus the Interpreter teaches him the method of interpreting life's situations, which becomes an invaluable resource as he later confronts situations whose meaning is not self-evident.

Stage 5. Beautiful Castle, Terrible Valleys

Proceeding on his journey, Christian has a series of experiences that, taken together, reflect the ambiguity of the adolescent stage of the life cycle. The first involves his overnight visit to Beautiful Castle, where he meets the four virgins Discretion, Prudence, Piety, and Charity. They listen to him as he tells of his travels. The next morning he continues on his way, beginning a long and arduous trek through the Valley of Humiliation and the Valley of the Shadow of Death.

In the first valley, he fights and finally subdues Apollyon, the monster who seeks to make him one of his subjects and who symbolizes pride. In the second, he comes to the very mouth of hell. After the two terrible ordeals, he comes to the end of the Valley of the Shadow of Death, where he meets Faithful, who joins him in his travel. Although Christian has met others on the road who have assisted him, this is his first real friendship.

In Christian's encounters, we see some of the turmoil, as well as the confusing mixture of positive and negative experiences, associated with adolescence. There are the emotional support and confirmation he receives from his conversations with the young women at Beautiful Castle, and the friendship that develops with Faithful. (Recall that fidelity is the saving virtue of this stage.) At the same time, as he proceeds through the two valleys, he experiences a severe testing of his faith and unrelenting personal abuse, and he witnesses the abject suffering of those who have lost their way and have come to a hellish end. The extremes of acceptance and abuse, confirmation and testing, friendship and alienation, intimate conversation and lonely ordeals, attraction and destruction are characteristic of the adolescent stage. Like the adolescent, Christian is forced to walk through narrow and dark valleys that allow little opportunity to anticipate and make appropriate preparation for the dangers that lurk there. The greatest danger is his confrontation with Apollyon, who symbolizes pride, the deadly sin of the adolescent era.

Stage 6. Vanity Fair

Accompanied by Faithful and two new companions, Talkative and Evangelist, Christian comes next to the town of Vanity, which has a fair that lasts all year long. When the four pilgrims arrive, they create a considerable hubbub because they are not attired like the other people. Accused of being mad, they are put into iron cages and publicly displayed, then tried and convicted for disturbing the peace. Faithful speaks in their defense, becoming the object of the jury's wrath, and is condemned to death. Christian is imprisoned but manages to escape. As he leaves Vanity Fair, he is joined by a new companion, Hopeful.

Christian's experiences at Vanity Fair correspond to the stage of young adulthood, because they bring him face to face with society, with its conflicts, passions, and lusts. Christian and his companions are persons of peace, but because they refuse to engage in the same self-aggrandizing behavior of the other people at the fair, they are accused of being disturbers of the peace. (We recall that the beatitude for this stage is "Blessed are the peacemakers. . . .") So Vanity Fair portrays the situation of the young adult who on entering the social world is faced with difficult choices in values, commitments, and life goals. Like the previous stage, this is a time of severe testing, but the struggle is not against the monster within us but against intense social pressures to make one's peace with a fallen world. The struggle here is not against self-pride but against social conventions. Yet as Faithful's tragic end reveals, the dangers are just as real and just as deadly. Christian and his friends reject the lusts reflected in Vanity Fair, but they pay a heavy price in terms of social condemnation. They are lust's victims.

Stage 7. Doubting Castle

Having escaped the town of Vanity, Christian, accompanied by Hopeful, continues his journey until he comes to Doubting Castle, the home of Giant Despair and his wife, Diffidence. Giant Despair casts them into prison without food, drink, or light, from Wednesday to Saturday night. He tries every way he knows to destroy their will to live, but the two travelers, though weak and disheartened, will not give up. They remain hopeful that relief will eventually come. At last, on Saturday night at midnight, Christian remembers that he has a key, called Promise, and he tries the key in the dungeon door. It unlocks with ease, allowing them to escape and continue their journey.

Doubting Castle corresponds to the stage of adulthood, because it symbolizes the apathy and indifference of the adult stage. For four days, Christian and Hopeful come close to giving up, nearly relinquishing the vision that has sustained them in their travels and accepting their imprisonment in Doubting Castle. But they do not lose heart, and eventually Christian realizes that the means of escape has been in his possession all along. What this says, in effect, is that the answer to the middle adult's apathy is not a new truth or new discovery but the rediscovery of an old truth that is able to break the bonds of incipient despair. With that rediscovery comes a liberated spirit, a new freedom that the Interpreter's caged man will never experience, because he is unable to repent and thereby enable the spirit of God to reenter his life and once again dwell in his soul. But Christian and Hopeful are able to escape because they have the key that could free them from their imprisonment. They do not gain their release by attempting to break through the iron bars that contain them. Instead their release comes with ease when they avail themselves of the key

they have possessed all along. And so it is with apathy and indifference. Release from these sins does not come from attempting to overcome them by means of our own strength. Rather, it comes from recognizing that the key to our release lies outside us and yet is well
within our reach.

Stage 8. Enchanted Ground

As Christian and Hopeful go on their way, leaving Doubting Castle
and Giant Despair behind, they cross over the Delectable Mountains,
from which they can view the Celestial City. Then they enter the Enchanted Ground. Now they are on land that belongs to the King of Celestial City, but they are not yet out of danger. The danger of Enchanted Ground is complacency, the false impression that a pilgrim
who has come this far has nothing further to fear. As Christian and
Hopeful travel through Enchanted Ground, they encounter various
false guides and are joined and then abandoned by weak companions.
But the greatest danger of all is drowsiness, the desire to sleep and
never rise again. Christian and Hopeful fight their drowsiness through
"good discourse," reflecting on the ways in which the spirit of God has
begun to work in each of them. Much of their conversation centers on
their common experience of Faithful and on his influence in their
lives. Their conversations keep them awake as they walk through Enchanted Ground to the River Jordan.

Christian's experience in Enchanted Ground relates to the eighth
life stage, because at this point in his journey the key to his ability to
keep his vision is his reflections on the past. These reflections give coherence and meaning to the journey thus far, and renewed anticipation of the goal that lies before him. As he and Hopeful talk, they are
especially mindful of their love for Faithful, which in turn strengthens
the bond between the two of them. Thus their reflections are not
mere reminiscences but are confirmations of the wisdom of the
course they have taken, of its essential integrity. They have lost Christian's friend Faithful, but they have "kept the faith."

Stage 9. The Celestial City

As Christian and Hopeful swim across the Jordan, Christian nearly
drowns. But Hopeful holds Christian's head above the water and they
manage to swim ashore locked in each other's arms. As they proceed
to the gate of Celestial City, they are accompanied by two men in shin-
ing white robes who have been sent to minister to them. As they approach the city, the King commands that they be allowed to enter.

Amid trumpet sounds they enter the city, and their pilgrimage is over. Christian and Hopeful have endured one last crisis, the crisis that we all undergo as the eighth stage ends and we confront not just the shadow but the reality of death.

The Pilgrimage in the Perspective of the Life Cycles

This brief account of Christian's pilgrimage shows that there are enough similarities between his encounters and the life-cycle stages to allow us to view the life cycle as a pilgrimage involving the dialectic of sin and salvation. Throughout his journey, Christian encounters persons whose names reflect various deadly sins and saving virtues, and he has experiences in which sin and virtue struggle against each other. His pilgrimage involves a continuing battle against the deadly sins and a continuing appropriation of the saving virtues. Being a keeper of the faith does not mean achieving moral or spiritual perfection. There is simply no way we can overcome sin once and for all in the course of our lives. But being a keeper of the faith means learning to discriminate between the voices and influences that lead to sin and those that lead to salvation. For this, Christian's sojourn in the Interpreter's house is especially important, because that is where he first learns to differentiate those who speak the truth from those who speak falsely. Were he not to learn this, he would not make the right friendships, which, as we have seen, are essential to the completion of his pilgrimage.

At the beginning of this chapter, I said that I hoped to revitalize the pilgrimage model by linking it to Erikson's life-cycle theory. There is probably no way to test directly whether the effort to place *The Pilgrim's Progress* within the life-cycle framework has succeeded in this regard. But one way to test it indirectly is to take up the more common criticisms of the pilgrimage motif and see if our approach here has helped to reduce those problems.

In *Requiem for a Lost Piety,* Edward Farley concludes that the problem with the pilgrimage model of Christian piety is its individualism, perfectionism, and inflexibility.[2] By individualism, he means that the model emphasizes the individual pilgrim who is intent on his or her own goal. By perfectionism, he means that the pilgrimage model takes a means-ends approach to the Christian life: "To attain B, do A; to be a Christian, do the following; to live a devout and holy life, engage in these disciplines."[3] By inflexibility, he means that the pilgrimage model has a fixed goal and this makes it difficult to respond to the living Word of God or to new and complex situations. Furthermore, "it appears that the twentieth-century Christian simply has no clear goal toward which the Christian life leads, the pursuing of which gives point to his religious activities."[4] Farley concludes that the vestiges of Protestant piety that are still around function outside the framework of the pilgrimage.

It would be nearly impossible to eliminate completely these three characteristics or tendencies from the pilgrimage model. In the final analysis, the pilgrimage model *is* goal-directed, with the desire to be with God being the fixed and immutable goal of the pilgrimage. That feature of the model is inescapably present and, in my judgment, is essential to it.

But whether this entails individualism, perfectionism, and inflexibility is another story. The individualistic tendency of the model is at least muted by Bunyan's (and my own) emphasis on the friendships that Christian makes along the way. Largely through conversation, the pilgrims discover that they have a common goal, and on this basis, they assist one another and sacrifice for one another. Since in Farley's later writings hospitality to the stranger is a key element of *ecclesia*, it may also be possible to see in the reception that Christian receives at the Interpreter's house and at Beautiful Castle an incipient model of *ecclesia*.[5] There is a clear emphasis on the individual in the pilgrimage model, but this does not entail an individualism.

The perfectionist tendency is also present here, as it is too in our discussion of the pilgrimage model in the first eight books of the Bible. There is a sense in which the model asserts that some "progress" is being made in the struggle against sin. But by placing the discussion of the pilgrimage motif in the context of the life-cycle theory and the dialectic between deadly sin and saving virtue, I am emphasizing that the struggle with sin is never concluded. If anything, sin becomes a more devilish problem as we grow older, because our repertoire for sin becomes more complex and multifaceted, which allows us, for example, to disguise our more serious sins by revealing or acknowledging lesser ones. Bunyan's description of Christian's journey, especially of his experiences in the Enchanted Ground and the crossing of the Jordan River, certainly establishes that, for the pilgrimage model, the traveler is always spiritually at risk. We cannot consider ourselves safe from sin until the final trumpet sounds. This is certainly the point, as well, of our attempt to correlate life stages and deadly sins.

The problem of inflexibility is a more difficult issue, because there can be a real question whether we are able to respond fully to the word of God en route if we are already certain of our destination. And are we free to "come to grips with new and complex situations" in life, including the "bursting forth of hitherto unimaginable possibilities and crises," if we are locked by a predetermined goal into a "fixed circle of duties and virtues"?[6] By viewing the life cycle as a series of crises that are present from the outset and inevitable, and by suggesting that the deadly sins and saving virtues are in some sense chronologically ordered, we have no doubt constructed a view of the pilgrimage as having a certain predetermined and hence inflexible character. But I think it is important to distinguish between a pilgrimage and a quest and to recognize that the pilgrimage has a greater sense of continuity and directedness than the quest.

Erikson has been criticized for his emphasis on the life cycle as an orderly process, especially by Robert Jay Lifton, who argues for a much more disorderly, discontinuous process.[7] Erikson acknowledges that he has a personal predisposition to be "enamored with the aesthetic order of things" and that this predisposition is reflected in his life-cycle theory.[8] But to critics who say that "all these neat listings" of life stages are merely Erikson's "ceremonial assurances" of an order that exists only in his own mind, he suggests that the order is there to see for those who have eyes to see. For him, the life cycle is an orderly process, a reflection of the "orderly harmony" that exists in the universe as a whole. So the question of inflexibility finally comes down to what it is that we see when we look around us. The pilgrim, unlike the quester, affirms a "visible world order as well as the orderliness of vision."[9] And this affirmation may in fact make the pilgrim *more* receptive to the living word of God and *more* open to hitherto unimaginable possibilities and crises.

The Bible as Pilgrim's Promise

In this and the preceding chapter, I have pointed to resources that are available to us in our struggles against the deadly sins. The resources are not precepts, rules, or principles, but words, images, metaphors, themes, stories, and motifs. The battle against the deadly sins is not waged through the force of a precept but by the power of the living word. As Luther suggests in his famous hymn "A Mighty Fortress Is Our God," the prince of darkness is not invincible, for indeed "One little word shall fell him." By choosing to focus on words, images, metaphors, themes, stories, and motifs, I have come down on the side of ethicists who argue that the moral life is not a matter of formulating principles and acting upon them but a way of seeing, of envisioning and revisioning the world and our place and purpose within it.[10] But though this study, by virtue of its subject matter, has many connections with "visional ethics," my concern has not been to take an ethical position of one sort or another but only to show that the Bible—the living Word of God—is still a powerful ally for us in our moral and spiritual struggles.

Of course, the Bible is not a talisman that has magical powers to dispel evil forces. We cannot hold the Bible up and expect it to wave our sins away. But the Bible does have the power to change lives. Through human history, it has proved for many to be the key called Promise which has the power to free us from sin's iron cage. Like the key called Promise, it has always been there, but many of us have forgotten that we knew we had it. May it be a means of release and empowerment as we make our pilgrimage together, laying aside every weight and sin that clings so closely, and looking to Jesus, the pioneer and perfecter of our faith.

Notes

Introduction

1. See Donald Capps, *Biblical Approaches to Pastoral Counseling* (Philadelphia: Westminster Press, 1981), 141–44; and idem, *Life Cycle Theory and Pastoral Care* (Philadelphia: Fortress Press, 1983), 104–6.

1. The Traditional Deadly Sins

1. Kenneth Slack, *The Seven Deadly Sins: A Contemporary View* (London: SCM Press, 1985), 1.
2. Geoffrey Chaucer, *The Canterbury Tales* (New York: Avenel Books, 1985). See also the edition translated by Nevill Coghill (New York: Viking Penguin, 1977).
3. Karl Menninger, *Whatever Became of Sin?* (New York: Hawthorn Books, 1973), 133–72.
4. Seward Hiltner, *Theological Dynamics* (Nashville: Abingdon Press, 1972), 93–94.
5. Stanford M. Lyman, *The Seven Deadly Sins: Society and Evil* (New York: St. Martin's Press, 1978).
6. Slack, *The Seven Deadly Sins*, 23–26, 34–36.
7. Judith N. Shklar, *Ordinary Vices* (Cambridge: Belknap Press of Harvard Univ. Press, 1984); Mary Daly, *Gyn/Ecology: The Metaethics of Radical Feminism* (Boston: Beacon Press, 1978); and idem, *Pure Lust* (Boston: Beacon Press, 1984).
8. Shklar, *Ordinary Vices*, 248.
9. Daly, *Gyn/Ecology*, 30–31.

2. The Sins of Infancy and Early Childhood

1. Erik H. Erikson, *Childhood and Society*, 2d rev. ed. (New York: W. W. Norton & Co., 1963 [1950]).

2. Donald Capps, *Life Cycle Theory and Pastoral Care* (Philadelphia: Fortress Press, 1983), chap. 1.

3. Carol Gilligan, *In a Different Voice* (Cambridge: Harvard Univ. Press, 1982), 11–13.

4. Brian W. Grant, *From Sin to Wholeness* (Philadelphia: Westminster Press, 1982).

5. Lance Webb, *Conquering the Seven Deadly Sins* (Nashville: Abingdon Press, 1955).

6. Basing his novel on the Jewish Holocaust of World War II, Stefan Kanfer suggests that the eighth sin is forgetting. See his *The Eighth Sin* (New York: Berkley Pub. Corp., 1978).

7. Henry Fairlie, *The Seven Deadly Sins Today* (Notre Dame, Ind.: Univ. of Notre Dame Press, 1979), 157.

8. Ibid., 167.

9. Kenneth Slack, *The Seven Deadly Sins: A Contemporary View* (London: SCM Press, 1985), 66.

10. Erik H. Erikson, *Identity and the Life Cycle* (New York: W. W. Norton & Co., 1959), 65–66.

11. Frances L. Ilg and Louise Bates Ames, *Child Behavior* (New York: Harper & Row, 1955), 23–26.

12. Erikson, *Identity and the Life Cycle,* 66.

13. Ilg and Ames, *Child Behavior,* 22.

14. Erikson, *Identity and the Life Cycle,* 66.

15. Erik H. Erikson, *Identity: Youth and Crisis* (New York: W. W. Norton & Co., 1968), 110.

16. Erikson, *Identity and the Life Cycle,* 70.

17. Stanford M. Lyman, *The Seven Deadly Sins: Society and Evil* (New York: St. Martin's Press, 1978), 114.

3. The Sins of the Play Age and School Age

1. Erik H. Erikson, *Identity: Youth and Crisis* (New York: W. W. Norton & Co., 1968), 115.

2. Erik H. Erikson, *Identity and the Life Cycle* (New York: W. W. Norton & Co., 1959), 81.

3. Ibid., 80.

4. Ibid.

5. Erikson, *Identity: Youth and Crisis,* 119–20.

6. Henry Fairlie, *The Seven Deadly Sins Today* (Notre Dame, Ind.: Univ. of Notre Dame Press, 1979), 135.

7. Stanford M. Lyman, *The Seven Deadly Sins: Society and Evil* (New York: St. Martin's Press, 1978), 232–33.

8. Fairlie, *The Seven Deadly Sins Today,* 147.

9. Kenneth Slack, *The Seven Deadly Sins: A Contemporary View* (London: SCM Press, 1985), 29.

10. Lyman, *The Seven Deadly Sins,* 263.

11. Erikson, *Identity and the Life Cycle,* 86.

12. Erikson, *Identity: Youth and Crisis,* 126.

13. Fairlie, *The Seven Deadly Sins Today,* 65; and Slack, *The Seven Deadly Sins,* 52.

14. Lyman, *The Seven Deadly Sins,* 186.

4. The Sins of Adolescence and Young Adulthood

1. The following discussion of the identity crisis is based on Erik H. Erikson's introductory chapter in his *Identity: Youth and Crisis* (New York: W. W. Norton & Co., 1968).

2. Ibid., 216–21.

3. Ibid., 29–30.

4. Erik H. Erikson, *Identity and the Life Cycle* (New York: W. W. Norton & Co., 1959), 91; and idem, *Identity: Youth and Crisis,* 132.

5. Erikson, *Identity: Youth and Crisis,* 216–21. See also Erik H. Erikson, "The Galilean Sayings and the Sense of 'I,'" *Yale Review* 70 (1981): 321–62.

6. See Paul C. Vitz, *Psychology as Religion: The Cult of Self-Worship* (Grand Rapids: Wm. B. Eerdmans, 1977).

7. Erikson, *Identity and the Life Cycle,* 89.

8. Henry Fairlie, *The Seven Deadly Sins Today* (Notre Dame, Ind.: Univ. of Notre Dame Press, 1979), 39.

9. Stanford M. Lyman, *The Seven Deadly Sins: Society and Evil* (New York: St. Martin's Press, 1978), 135.

10. Fairlie, *The Seven Deadly Sins Today,* 44–45.

11. Ibid., 48.

12. Ibid.

13. Lyman, *The Seven Deadly Sins,* 155.

14. Erikson, *Identity: Youth and Crisis,* 220.

15. Erik H. Erikson, *Childhood and Society,* 2d rev. ed. (New York: W. W. Norton & Co., 1963 [1950]), 263.

16. Ibid., 266.

17. Fairlie, *The Seven Deadly Sins Today,* 175.

18. Ibid.

19. Kenneth Slack, *The Seven Deadly Sins: A Contemporary View* (London: SCM Press, 1985), 48.

20. Lyman, *The Seven Deadly Sins,* 77.

21. Ibid., 80.

22. James M. Gustafson, "The Minister as Moral Counselor," *Journal of Psychology and Christianity* 3 (1984): 16.

5. The Sins of Middle and Mature Adulthood

1. Erik H. Erikson, *Identity: Youth and Crisis* (New York: W. W. Norton & Co., 1968), 138–39.

2. Ibid., 139.

3. Erik H. Erikson, *Childhood and Society,* 2d rev. ed. (New York: W. W. Norton & Co., 1963 [1950]), 267–68.

4. Ibid., 267.

5. Henry Fairlie, *The Seven Deadly Sins Today* (Notre Dame, Ind.: Univ. of Notre Dame Press, 1979), 113.

6. Stanford M. Lyman, *The Seven Deadly Sins: Society and Evil* (New York: St. Martin's Press, 1978), 8–10, 14–18.

7. Dorothy Sayers, quoted by Fairlie in *The Seven Deadly Sins Today,* 114.

8. Erik H. Erikson, *Young Man Luther* (New York: W. W. Norton & Co., 1958), 213–14.

9. Erikson, *Identity: Youth and Crisis,* 261–94.

10. Erikson, *Childhood and Society,* 268.

11. Erikson, *Identity: Youth and Crisis,* 139.

12. Erikson, *Childhood and Society,* 268.

13. Erikson, *Identity: Youth and Crisis,* 139.

14. Erik H. Erikson, *The Life Cycle Completed* (New York: W. W. Norton & Co., 1982), 65.

15. Ibid.

16. Erik H. Erikson, *Identity and the Life Cycle* (New York: W. W. Norton & Co., 1959), 98.

17. Erikson, *The Life Cycle Completed,* 63.

18. Ibid., 65.

19. Fairlie, *The Seven Deadly Sins Today,* 125.

20. Lyman, *The Seven Deadly Sins,* 11.

21. Ibid., 12–13.

22. Richard K. Fenn, *Liturgies and Trials* (New York: Pilgrim Press, 1982), 107–8.

6. The Virtues of Infancy and Early Childhood

1. Erik H. Erikson, *Insight and Responsibility* (New York: W. W. Norton & Co., 1964), 111–57.

2. Ibid., 111–12.

3. Ibid., 113.

4. Ibid., 118.

5. Ibid.

6. Erik H. Erikson, *Gandhi's Truth* (New York: W. W. Norton & Co., 1968), 415–16.

7. The Virtues of Childhood and Adolescence

1. Erik H. Erikson, *Insight and Responsibility* (New York: W. W. Norton & Co., 1964), 120.

2. Ibid., 122.

3. Ibid., 123.

4. Ibid., 123–24.

5. Erik H. Erikson, *Young Man Luther* (New York: W. W. Norton & Co., 1958), 192.

6. Erikson, *Insight and Responsibility*, 125.
7. Ibid., 126.
8. Ibid., 125.

8. The Virtues of Adulthood

1. Erik H. Erikson, *Insight and Responsibility* (New York: W. W. Norton & Co., 1964), 127–28.
2. Ibid., 129.
3. Ibid., 130.
4. Ibid., 129.
5. Ibid., 130–31.
6. Ibid., 130.
7. Ibid., 131.
8. Ibid.
9. Ibid., 132.
10. Ibid., 133.
11. Ibid., 134.
12. Ibid., 133.
13. Ibid.
14. Ibid., 134.
15. Ibid., 133.
16. Ibid., 134.
17. Ibid.

9. The Beatitudes—Elements of an Active Faith

1. Erik H. Erikson, "The Galilean Sayings and the Sense of 'I,'" *Yale Review* 70 (1981): 321–62.
2. William Barclay, *The Beatitudes and the Lord's Prayer for Everyman* (New York: Harper & Row, 1975), 11.
3. See Robert Schuller, *The Be (Happy) Attitudes* (Waco, Tex.: Word Books, 1985).
4. Paul S. Minear, *Matthew: The Teacher's Gospel* (New York: Pilgrim Press, 1982), 46.
5. Myron S. Augsburger, *The Expanded Life* (Nashville: Abingdon Press, 1972).
6. See Donald Capps, "The Beatitudes and Erikson's Life Cycle Theory," *Pastoral Psychology* 33 (1985): 226–44.
7. Barclay, *The Beatitudes and the Lord's Prayer for Everyman*, 81.
8. Augsburger, *The Expanded Life*, 78, 84–85.
9. Paul W. Pruyser, "Maintaining Hope in Adversity," *Pastoral Psychology* 35 (1986): 123–24.
10. Barclay, *The Beatitudes and the Lord's Prayer for Everyman*, 41.
11. Ibid., 23.
12. Ibid., 115.

13. Augsburger, *The Expanded Life,* 96.

14. Barclay, *The Beatitudes and the Lord's Prayer for Everyman,* 87.

15. Clement of Alexandria, quoted by Barclay in ibid., 89.

16. Ibid., 30.

17. See Erik H. Erikson, *Dimensions of a New Identity* (New York: W. W. Norton & Co., 1974), 49. This quotation is from Erikson's "The Galilean Sayings and the Sense of 'I,'" 237.

10. Biblical Stories and the Pilgrim's Way

1. John Bunyan, *The Pilgrim's Progress* (New York: Washington Square Press, 1957).

2. Edward Farley, *Requiem for a Lost Piety* (Philadelphia: Westminster Press, 1966), 86–88.

3. Ibid., 87.

4. Ibid., 90.

5. Edward Farley, *Ecclesial Man: A Social Phenomenology of Faith and Reality* (Philadelphia: Fortress Press, 1975), 169–74.

6. Farley, *Requiem for a Lost Piety,* 87.

7. Robert Jay Lifton, "Protean Man," *Partisan Review* 35 (1968): 13–27.

8. Erik H. Erikson, *Life History and the Historical Moment* (New York: W. W. Norton & Co., 1975), 31.

9. Erik H. Erikson, *Toys and Reasons* (New York: W. W. Norton & Co., 1977), 126.

10. See, e.g., Stanley Hauerwas, *Vision and Virtue* (Notre Dame, Ind.: Univ. of Notre Dame Press, 1981); Craig R. Dykstra, *Vision and Character* (Ramsey, N.J.: Paulist Press, 1981); and Karen LeBacqz, *Professional Ethics* (Nashville: Abingdon Press, 1985).

Index

Abel, 42, 138
Abstinence, temperance, and
    sobriety, 74, 81
Adam and Eve, 50, 138, 140–42
Aggression, 29–30, 50
Alcuin, 23
Ames, Louise Bates, 28
Anger, 11–12, 18, 22, 28, 30–31, 74,
    83–86, 105, 126
Anxiety, 23
Apathy (*acedia*), 12, 41, 58–63,
    68–70, 101, 107–10, 116, 133,
    147–48
Aquinas, 54
Aristotle, 19, 125
Augsburger, Myron S., 124, 126,
    129–30
Augustine, 54.
Autonomy, v. shame and doubt, 21,
    28–31, 65, 81, 135

Balaam, 90–91, 100
Barclay, William, 124–26, 129–35
Basic trust v. basic mistrust, 21, 25,
    27, 79–81, 93, 125, 135
Beatitudes, 6, 57, 119–21, 123–24,
    130, 132, 134–37, 142
    concerning the meek, 123, 125–26
    concerning the merciful, 123,
        132–33

concerning the peacemakers, 123,
    131–32, 146
concerning the poor in spirit, 123,
    128–29
concerning the pure in heart,
    123–25
concerning those who are
    persecuted, 123, 129–30
concerning those who hunger and
    thirst for righteousness, 123,
    126–28, 129
concerning those who mourn, 123,
    133–34
Beauty, 26, 28
Bible, 57, 63, 119, 138, 144, 150–52
    use of, 5, 75, 77, 120, 138
Bunyan, John, 6, 137, 142, 150
    Beautiful Castle, 145, 150
    Celestial City, 148, 150
    City of Destruction, 142
    Doubting Castle, 147
    Enchanted Ground, 148, 150
    Interpreter's house, 145, 150
    Morality Village, 144
    Slough of Despond, 144
    Vanity Fair, 146

Cain, 42–43, 138, 141
Capps, Donald, 22

Care, 19, 76, 101, 104, 106, 108, 110, 115–16, 133, 134–35
Chastity and continence, 74, 106
Chaucer, 11, 13, 19, 23, 26, 30, 35, 40, 49, 53, 74, 80, 85, 90, 95
Church, 55
Commitment, 51–52, 102–3, 105, 146
Competence, 19, 76
and discipline, 76, 87, 91–94, 99, 103–4, 129, 135
Conscience, 35, 39, 88–89, 91, 144
Constancy, 99–100, 115–16, 120, 141
Continuity, 99–100, 103, 115–16
Crisis points, 2–3, 21–23, 28, 151
negative pole, 21, 23, 29, 34, 38, 48–49, 53, 55, 58, 65, 102
positive pole, 21, 25, 29, 34, 41, 49, 55, 58, 64, 112
Cruelty, 16–17, 54, 56, 103

Daly, Mary, 16–18, 77
Dante, 11
Deadly sins, 2, 13, 28, 30, 36, 48, 52, 56–57, 59–60, 66, 68, 73–74, 77, 83, 86, 88, 91, 93–95, 101–2, 104, 106, 108, 112, 116, 119, 131, 135, 137, 141, 149, 151
adequacy of list of, 16
classification of, 16
and the developmental process, 3, 18, 22, 26, 31, 37, 41, 44, 46, 48, 51, 52–53, 55, 58–59, 62–64, 66–67, 73, 75, 80, 102, 110, 112, 119
diagnostic use, 19
and dispositions, 15, 23, 32, 42, 44, 50, 55, 56, 59, 62, 66, 69, 79, 80–81, 86, 110, 112, 119
eight, 12, 22, 70, 74
seven, 11, 22, 74
and social evil, 15–16, 18, 43, 50–51, 54–56, 60–61, 91, 105
and women, 17–18
Deuteronomy, 140
Discrimination, 27–28, 79–80, 149

Emulation, 43–44
Envy, 11–12, 18, 22, 33, 35, 39–41, 43–45, 74, 87, 93–95, 105
Erikson, Erik, 3–5, 7, 19, 21, 25, 28–29, 37–39, 42–43, 46–49, 52–53, 58, 63–65, 74–77, 79, 81–82, 86–88, 91–93, 95, 101–4, 106–12, 115, 119–20, 124, 134–35, 136, 140, 142, 149, 151
Esau, 80, 86
Evagrius of Pontus, 12
Exodus, 138

Fairlie, Henry, 30, 35–36, 40, 49–51, 53–54, 66
Faith, 120–21, 134
elements of, 121, 123, 136
and empathy, 123, 132–33
and equity, 123, 126–27
and expectancy, 123–25
and longing, 123, 133–34
and nonconformity, 123, 129–30
and peacemaking, 123, 130–32, 146
and self-mastery, 123, 125–26
and self-worth, 123, 128–29
Farley, Edward, 149–50
Fenn, Richard, 69
Fidelity, 19, 76, 87, 95, 98–100, 103–4, 130, 135, 141, 146
Fortitude, 74, 110
Freud, Sigmund, 47–48, 67

Generativity v. stagnation, 21, H2–53, 58–59, 62–66, 69, 107–9, 116, 135
Genesis, 137, 142
Gluttony, 11, 18, 22, 25–27, 32, 35, 40, 45, 53, 74, 79–81, 85
God, 3, 43, 52, 54, 61, 63, 77, 84, 98, 104, 106, 108–9, 114, 116, 124–29, 131–35, 141, 150–51
Grant, Brian W., 22
Greed, 11–12, 18, 22, 25–27, 32, 35, 40, 45, 53, 74, 79–81, 85–86, 125
Gregory the Great, 12, 23, 66

Hamlet, 67
Hiltner, Seward, 14–15
Holy Spirit, 12, 63
Hope, 19, 61, 76–77, 79–81; 85–86,
    91, 99, 103–4, 124–25, 135,
    141, 146
Humility, 74, 99

Identity v. identity confusion, 21,
    46–49, 51–53, 66, 101–5,
    133–35
Ilg, Francis L., 28
Image of God, 4
Industry v. inferiority, 21, 33, 39–43,
    92, 95, 128–29, 135
Initiative v. guilt, 21, 33–34, 37–38,
    65, 88, 135
Integrity v. despair, 21, 52, 58,
    63–66, 68, 111, 113–15, 135,
    147
Intimacy v. isolation, 21, 46, 52–53,
    55, 66, 101–6, 131, 135

James, William, 33, 47–48
Jesus, 135–36, 152
Job, 113–15
John of Cassian, 12–13
Jonah, 98–100
Joshua, 140
Judges, 140

Koheleth, 109

Leviticus, 138
Life-cycle theory and stages, 21, 23,
    46, 58, 63–65, 74–76, 106,
    110–11, 116, 119, 121, 124,
    134–35, 138, 142, 149–51
  infancy, 21, 25, 29, 73, 77, 81, 86,
    100, 124–26, 140, 144
  early childhood, 21, 28, 30–31, 73,
    81, 86, 100, 125–26, 140, 144
  play age, 33–34, 37, 39, 87–89,
    99–100, 127, 140, 144–45
  school age, 33, 39, 42, 87, 91–92,
    99–100, 128–29, 140, 145
  adolescence, 46–47, 51, 87, 95,
    99–100, 108, 129–30, 140, 145

  young adulthood, 46–47, 52–53,
    55, 101–2, 106, 108, 116, 131,
    140, 146
  middle adulthood, 58, 68, 101,
    106–8, 110, 116, 133, 140, 147
  mature adulthood, 58, 63, 65, 67,
    69, 101, 110, 112–13, 115–16,
    134, 140, 148
Lifton, Robert J., 151
Love, 19, 53–54, 64, 68, 74, 76, 95,
    101–7, 112, 115–16, 132, 135,
    141
Lust, 11–12, 18, 22, 46, 52–56, 74,
    101–6, 115, 131–32
Luther, Martin, 54–55, 63, 151
Lyman, Stanford, 15, 18, 26, 30, 35,
    41, 49, 51, 54, 60–61, 66

Melancholy (*tristitia*), 12, 23, 58, 63,
    66–70, 74, 101, 112–14
Menninger, Karl, 14–16
Mercy, 74, 90
Miller, Arthur, 48
Minear, Paul, 123, 132
Montaigne, 16–17
Moral selfhood, 99–100, 115
Moses, 84, 86

Narcissism, 51, 56
Numbers, 138

Ordinary vices, 16

Parables, 36, 42–43, 83
Patience, 74, 85
Paul, 19
Pilgrim motif, 6–7, 120, 137–38,
    140, 142, 149–52
Plato, 125
Pride, 11–12, 18, 22, 35, 42, 46,
    48–52, 55–56, 70, 74, 87,
    98–99, 141, 146
Pruyser, Paul W., 125
Puritans, 54, 56
Purpose, 19, 76, 88–9^
  and dedication, 76, 88–89, 91, 99,
    104, 127, 135

Responsibility, 39, 64, 103, 109–10
Righteousness, 41
Ruth, 105, 137–38, 140–42

Samson, 104
Saul, 94–95, 100
Saving virtues, 3, 20, 73, 77, 81, 83, 85–87, 91, 94–95, 101, 103–4, 106, 110, 115–16, 119–21, 127, 133, 135, 137, 140–41, 149
  definition of, 4
  developmental, 4, 73, 75, 77, 80, 87, 91–92, 95, 99–101, 110, 115, 119
  and dispositions, 4–5, 73, 77, 79–82, 86, 93, 95, 99–100, 108, 110, 115, 119–21
Self-esteem, 49, 85, 98
Self-indulgence, 59, 63
Shklar, Judith, 16–18
Sin, 1, 70, 84, 90, 138, 150, 152
  as attitude, 2
  cultural, 19
  developmental, 3
  dispositional, 1–2, 32, 50
  as impulse, 2
  as isolation, 15, 32, 41, 44–45, 50–51, 56, 69–70, 98–99, 116, 141

as missing the mark, 15, 22
  and personal bondage, 15, 32, 44, 50–51, 56, 69–70, 116, 141
  as rebellion, 15, 32, 44, 50, 52, 56, 69–70, 116, 141
  and salvation, 138, 140, 142, 149
Slack, Kenneth, 15, 18, 26, 36, 40, 54
Sloth, 11–12, 18, 22–23, 59–61, 74, 110
Spock, Benjamin, 28, 31

Virtues, 3, 73–75, 77, 81–82, 87–88, 90, 92, 101–2, 105, 138
  cultivation of, 5, 19, 57, 119
  as dispositions, 4–5
Vitality, 115–16, 120, 141

Webb, Lance, 23
Will, 19, 28–29, 63, 76, 82
  and courage, 76, 81–86, 90, 99, 103–4, 108, 125–26, 134–35
Williams, Harry, 54
Wisdom, 19, 76, 101, 104, 109–16, 134–35, 141
World, 85–86, 89–91, 109, 114–16, 120, 141, 142, 152